# CASE STUDIES IN NOT-FOR-PROFIT ACCOUNTING AND AUDITING

BY BRUCE CHASE, PH.D., CPA; LAURA LINDAL, CPA;
WILLIAM WAGNER, CPA

## Notice to Readers

*Case Studies in Not-For-Profit Accounting and Auditing* is intended solely for use in continuing professional education and not as a reference. It does not represent an official position of the American Institute of Certified Public Accountants, and it is distributed with the understanding that the author and publisher are not rendering legal, accounting, or other professional services in the publication. This course is intended to be an overview of the topics discussed within, and the author has made every attempt to verify the completeness and accuracy of the information herein. However, neither the author nor publisher can guarantee the applicability of the information found herein. If legal advice or other expert assistance is required, the services of a competent professional should be sought.

> **You can qualify to earn free CPE through our pilot testing program.**
> **If interested, please visit aicpa.org at http://apps.aicpa.org/secure/CPESurvey.aspx.**

Course Code: **745216**
CNFP GS-0416-0B
Revised: **May 2016**

# TABLE OF CONTENTS

Users of this course material are encouraged to visit the AICPA website at www.aicpa.org/CPESupplements to access supplemental learning material reflecting recent developments that may be applicable to this course. The AICPA anticipates that supplemental materials will be made available on a quarterly basis.

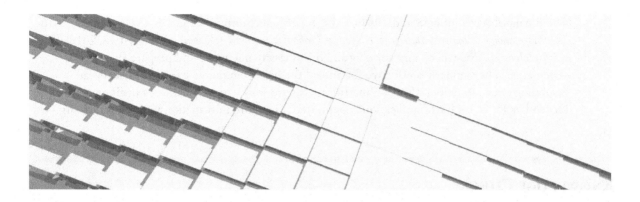

## Chapter 1

# FINANCIAL STATEMENT REQUIREMENTS

## LEARNING OBJECTIVES

After completing this chapter, you should be able to do the following:

- Identify the basic financial statements.
- Determine the basic requirements of the financial statements.

## TECHNICAL BACKGROUND INFORMATION

In the list below, the FASB *Accounting Standards Codification* (ASC) 958, *Not-for-Profit Entities*, requires not-for-profit entities (NFPs) to present financial statements showing aggregate information about the entity. The general-purpose financial statements required by FASB ASC 958 also include the accompanying notes to the financial statements.

The general-purpose financial statements required by FASB ASC 958 for not-for-profit entities are:

1. The Statement of Financial Position [May also properly be referred to as a Balance Sheet]

2. The Statement of Activities

3. The Statement of Cash Flows

4. Voluntary health and welfare organizations are also required to present a Statement of Functional Expenses

---

The Financial Accounting Standards Board's (FASB) Accounting Standards Update (ASU) 2016-14, *Presentation of Financial Statements of Not-for-Profit Entities*, was released on August 18, 2016. The newly released ASU will change the way all NFPs classify net assets and prepare financial statements. The standard is effective for annual financial statements issued for fiscal years beginning after December 15, 2017 and for interim periods within fiscal years beginning after December 15, 2018. Early application is permitted. For more information visit www.fasb.org.

## KNOWLEDGE CHECK

1. Which is true of the general-purpose financial statements for not-for-profit entities?

    a. Voluntary health and welfare organizations are required to present a Statement of Functional Expenses.
    b. Not-for-profit entities do not present financial statements showing aggregate information about the entity.
    c. The general-purpose financial statements exclude the accompanying notes to the financial statements.
    d. The general-purpose financial statements for not-for-profit organizations are the same as for businesses.

### The Statement of Financial Position

A statement of financial position reports an entity's assets, liabilities, and net assets. Generally, assets and liabilities should be aggregated into reasonably homogeneous groups. Assets need not be disaggregated based on the presence of donor-imposed restrictions on their use; for example, cash available for unrestricted current use need not be reported separately from cash received with donor-imposed restrictions that is also available for current use. However, cash or other assets either (*a*) designated for long-term purposes, or (*b*) received with donor-imposed restrictions that limit their use to long-term purposes should not be aggregated on a statement of financial position with cash or other assets that is available for current use. For example, cash that has been received with donor-imposed restrictions limiting its use to the acquisition of long-lived assets should be reported under a separate caption, such as "cash restricted to investment in property and equipment," and displayed near the section of the statement where property and equipment is displayed. The kind of asset should be described in the notes to the financial statements if its nature is not clear from the description on the face of the statement of financial position. As illustrated in the following, assets and liabilities can be presented in a number of ways to provide information about liquidity.

## APPROACHES TO PROVIDING INFORMATION ABOUT LIQUIDITY

▪ Sequencing assets according to their nearness of conversion to cash and sequencing liabilities according to the nearness of their maturity and resulting use of cash.
▪ Classifying assets and liabilities as current and noncurrent, as defined by the FASB ASC 210, *Balance Sheet*.
▪ Disclosing in notes to financial statements relevant information about the liquidity or maturity of assets and liabilities, including restrictions on the use of particular assets.

The statement of financial position should focus on the organization as a whole. It does this by reporting total assets, total liabilities, and total net assets for the organization. Three classes of net assets are required to be reported as unrestricted net assets, temporarily restricted net assets, or permanently restricted net assets.

Information about the nature and amounts of different types of permanent restrictions or temporary restrictions on net assets should be reported either on the face of the statement or in the notes to the financial statement. Separate lines in the statement may be used for permanently restricted net assets to distinguish between holdings (such as land or collections) and endowments.

Separate lines in the financial statements can also be used for temporarily restricted net assets to distinguish among the following types of donor restrictions: support of a particular operating activity, investment for a specified term, use in a specified period, or acquisition of a long-lived asset.

Unrestricted net assets can also use separate lines to report self-imposed limits (designations) on net assets. In cases where separate lines are used in any of the three classes of net assets, a total of aggregate net assets, the sum of all separately stated unrestricted, temporarily restricted, and permanently restricted net assets, must also be shown in the net assets section of the statement of financial position. Exhibit 1-1 reports one example of a statement of financial position. Note that this example sequences assets and liabilities based on liquidity and does not display information about the nature of restrictions on the face of the financial statement.

## KNOWLEDGE CHECK

2. Which is true of the statement of financial position?

    a. Information about the nature and amounts of different types of permanent restrictions or temporary restrictions on net assets should be either reported on the face of the statement or in the notes to the financial statement.
    b. Unrestricted net assets cannot use separate lines to report self-imposed limits (designations) on net assets.
    c. Assets and liabilities cannot be presented in a number of ways to provide information about liquidity.
    d. Totals are only required to be reported for net assets.

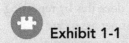

**Exhibit 1-1**

## Not-for-Profit "A"
## Statement of Financial Position
## June 30, 20X2 and 20X1
## (in thousands)

| | 20X2 | 20X1 |
|---|---|---|
| **Assets:** | | |
| Cash and cash equivalents | $ 85 | $ 560 |
| Accounts and interest receivable | 1,130 | 1,680 |
| Inventories and prepaid expenses | 710 | 1,020 |
| Contributions receivable | 3,025 | 2,700 |
| Short-term investments | 6,410 | 5,560 |
| Collections of works of art (Note X) | – | – |
| Land, buildings, and equipment | 60,600 | 63,580 |
| Long-term investments | 218,070 | 203,500 |
| Total assets | $290,030 | $278,600 |
| **Liabilities and net assets:** | | |
| Accounts payable | $ 2,070 | $ 1,150 |
| Refundable advance | 200 | 450 |
| Grants payable | 675 | 1,500 |
| Notes payable | 500 | 1,040 |
| Long-term debt | 7,185 | 8,200 |
| Total liabilities | 10,630 | 12,340 |
| **Net assets:** | | |
| Unrestricted | 113,138 | 103,770 |
| Temporarily restricted | 24,242 | 25,490 |
| Permanently restricted | 142,020 | 137,000 |
| Total net assets | 279,400 | 266,260 |
| Total liabilities and net assets | $290,030 | $278,600 |

## The Statement of Activities

In many ways, the statement of activities parallels an income statement for a for profit organization. However, because not-for-profit entities have an operating purpose other than making a profit, for profit financial statement terms, such as income statement and net income, are not used. Instead, the terms "statement of activities" and "change in net assets" are used in the reporting of NFPs.

The statement of activities focuses on the organization as a whole for a specified period of time (the current fiscal year) and requires that the amount of change in net assets for the period be reported. In addition, the amount of change in permanently restricted net assets, temporarily restricted net assets and unrestricted net assets must also be reported.

The statement of activities reports revenues, gains, expenses, and losses for the period. Revenues are reported as increases in unrestricted net assets unless the use of the assets received is limited by donor-imposed restrictions. Expenses are reported as decreases in unrestricted net assets. That may seem somewhat odd at first. However, as organizations use resources to meet donor-restricted purposes, the resources are released from restrictions and the expenses are reported as a decrease in unrestricted net assets. Likewise, gains and losses recognized on investments and other assets (or liabilities) are reported as increases or decreases in unrestricted net assets unless their use is temporarily or permanently restricted by explicit donor stipulations or by law.

An organization must report information about the functional classification of expenses, such as major classes of program services and supporting activities. This information can be done on the face of the statement of activities or in the notes to the financial statements. Therefore, organizations can display expenses either by natural or functional classification in the statement of activities as long as the functional information is presented.

Events that simultaneously increase one class of net assets and decrease another class of net assets (reclassifications) are reported as separate items in the statement of activities. For example, using resources to meet a temporary donor-stipulated restriction would simultaneously decrease temporarily restricted net assets and increase unrestricted net assets.

NFPs have a great deal of flexibility in how items are sequenced in the statement of activities. Revenues, gains, expenses, losses, and reclassifications can be arranged in a variety of orders. In addition, an organization may choose to report some intermediate measure of operations, such as operating revenues over operating expenses, to show margin.

Exhibit 1-2 reports one example of a statement of activities. Note that this example uses three columns to display information about the three classes of net assets. Also, note that change in net assets, as well as changes in the three classes of net assets, is reported. Reclassifications (net assets released from restrictions) are reported separately.

## KNOWLEDGE CHECK

3.  Which is true of the statement of activities?

    a.  The amount of change in permanently restricted net assets cannot be reported.
    b.  The amount of change in temporarily restricted net assets cannot be reported.
    c.  The amount of change in unrestricted net assets must be reported.
    d.  The amount of change net assets cannot be reported.

4.  Which is true of the statement of activities?

    a.  Events that simultaneously increase one class of net assets and decrease another class of net assets (reclassifications) are reported as separate items in the statement of activities.
    b.  Revenues, gains, expenses, losses, and reclassifications cannot be arranged in a variety of orders.
    c.  Revenue can only be reported as increases in unrestricted net assets.
    d.  Expenses must be displayed by natural classification in the statement of activities.

**Exhibit 1-2 Not-for-Profit "B" Statement of Activities Year Ended June 30, 20X3 (in thousands)**

| | Unrestricted | Temporarily Restricted | Permanently Restricted | Total |
|---|---|---|---|---|
| **Revenues, gains, and other support:** | | | | |
| Contributions | $ 8,790 | $ 9,100 | $ 380 | $ 18,270 |
| Fees | 5,600 | | | 5,600 |
| Income on long-term investments (Note F) | 5,200 | 1,590 | 120 | 6,910 |
| Other investment income (Note F) | 650 | | | 650 |
| Net unrealized and realized gains on long-term investments (Note F) | 8,628 | 2,952 | 4,520 | 16,100 |
| Net assets released from restrictions (Note E): | | | | |
| Satisfaction of program restrictions | 13,490 | (13,490) | | |
| Expiration of time restrictions | 1,250 | (1,250) | | |
| Total revenues, gains, and other support | 43,608 | (1,098) | 5,020 | 47,530 |
| **Expenses:** | | | | |
| Program 1 | 12,380 | | | 12,380 |
| Program 2 | 9,340 | | | 9,340 |
| Program 3 | 2,720 | | | 2,720 |
| Management and general | 5,460 | | | 5,460 |
| Fund raising | 4,150 | | | 4,150 |
| Total expenses (Note G) | 34,050 | | | 34,050 |
| Change in net assets | 9,558 | (1,098) | 5,020 | 13,480 |
| Net assets at beginning of year | 120,675 | 28,470 | 155,000 | 304,145 |
| Net assets at end of year | $130,233 | $27,372 | $160,020 | $317,625 |

FASB ASC 958-205-05-5 requires NFPs to report a statement of cash flows. Organizations should follow the provisions of the FASB ASC 230-10-45, *Statement of Cash Flows*.

The listing of financing activities in FASB ASC 230-10-45-14 includes cash receipts that are donor-restricted for long-term purposes. Examples include contributions for capital assets and additions to an endowment. However, because cash restricted for long-term purposes is normally excluded from cash available for current use, a cash contribution for a long-term purpose would normally be reported as both a cash inflow from financing activities and a cash outflow from investing activities.

Organizations may report cash flows from operating activities using either the direct or indirect method. Whereas, for business enterprises, cash flow activity is reconciled to net income (the starting point of the reconciliation) in the statement of cash flows, under the indirect method (as required by GAAP), NFPs reconcile cash flow activities to the change in total net assets (the starting point of the reconciliation) In addition, cash flow from operating activities would include, if applicable, agency transactions. Exhibit 1-3 presents an example statement of cash flows.

## KNOWLEDGE CHECK

5. Which is true of the statement of cash flows?

    a. Cash flow from operating activities would always exclude agency transactions.
    b. Because cash restricted for long-term purposes is normally excluded from cash available for current use, a cash contribution for a long-term purpose would normally be reported as both a cash inflow from financing activities and a cash outflow from investing activities.
    c. Cash flow for operating activities must be reported using the direct method.
    d. Using the direct method, NFP must reconcile cash flow activities to change in unrestricted net assets.

## Exhibit 1-3 Not-for-Profit "C" Statement of Cash Flows Year Ended June 30, 20X4 (in thousands)

| | |
|---|---:|
| Cash flows from operating activities: | |
| Change in net assets | $ 15,500 |
| Adjustments to reconcile change in net assets to net cash used by operating activities: | |
| Depreciation | 4,000 |
| Increase in accounts and interest receivable | (640) |
| Decrease in inventories and prepaid expenses | 290 |
| Increase in contributions receivable | (425) |
| Increase in accounts payable | 2,520 |
| Decrease in refundable advance | (450) |
| Decrease in grants payable | (400) |
| Contributions restricted for long-term investment | (3,540) |
| Interest and dividends restricted for long-term investment | (400) |
| Net unrealized and realized gains on long-term investments | (16,800) |
| Net cash used by operating activities | (345) |
| Cash flows from investing activities: | |
| Purchase of equipment | (1,500) |
| Proceeds from sale of investments | 70,000 |
| Purchase of investments | (78,200) |
| Net cash used by investing activities | (9,700) |
| Cash flows from financing activities: | |
| Proceeds from contributions restricted for: | |
| Investment in endowment | 300 |
| Investment in term endowment | 50 |
| Investment in plant | 1,300 |
| | 1,650 |
| Other financing activities: | |
| Interest and dividends restricted for reinvestment | 55 |
| Payments on notes payable | (1,040) |
| Payments on long-term debt | (1,100) |
| | (2,085) |
| Net cash used by financing activities | (435) |
| Net decrease in cash and cash equivalents | (10,480) |
| Cash and cash equivalents at beginning of year | 10,530 |
| Cash and cash equivalents at end of year | $ 50 |
| Supplemental data: | |
| Noncash investing and financing activities: | |
| Gifts of equipment | $ 240 |
| Gift of paid-up life insurance, cash surrender value | 50 |
| Interest paid | 521 |

FASB ASC 958-205-05-5 requires voluntary health and welfare organizations to report a fourth financial statement, a statement of functional expenses. Because these types of organizations depend primarily on contributions from the general public, the statement of functional expenses provides additional information on how resources are used. The statement of functional expenses uses a matrix format to report expenses by both functional and natural classification. Exhibit 1-4 is an example of a statement of functional expenses. This matrix format makes it easy to determine the extent to which resources are used for such things as salaries, travel, and supplies within a program area.

## KNOWLEDGE CHECK

6.  Which is true of voluntary health and welfare organizations?

    a.  Voluntary health and welfare organizations are not allowed to report a statement of functional expenses.
    b.  Voluntary health and welfare organizations depend primarily on contributions from the general public.
    c.  The statement of functional expenses does not provide any information on how resources are used.
    d.  The statement of functional expenses does not provide information on functional and natural classification of expenses.

## Exhibit 1-4 Not-for-Profit "D" Statement of Functional Expenses Year Ended June 30, 20X5 (in thousands)

| | Program | Supporting Services | | Total |
|---|---|---|---|---|
| | | Management and General | Fund Raising | |
| Awards and grants | $50,632 | $    — | $    — | $ 50,632 |
| Salaries | 2,720 | 9,471 | 12,076 | 24,267 |
| Employee benefits | 365 | 1,717 | 8,466 | 10,548 |
| Payroll taxes | 145 | 2,132 | 1,680 | 3,957 |
| Professional fees | 142 | 1,096 | 1,338 | 2,576 |
| Supplies | 72 | 628 | 1,618 | 2,318 |
| Telephone | 191 | 562 | 1,206 | 1,959 |
| Postage and shipping | 44 | 416 | 2,929 | 3,389 |
| Occupancy | 287 | 1,695 | 2,591 | 4,573 |
| Information processing | 656 | 562 | 1,549 | 2,767 |
| Printing and publications | 135 | 612 | 4,885 | 5,632 |
| Meetings and conferences | 719 | 1,085 | 2,167 | 3,971 |
| Other travel | 191 | 788 | 1,192 | 2,171 |
| Other expenses | 159 | 919 | 502 | 1,580 |
| Depreciation | 634 | 913 | 1,534 | 3,081 |
| Total expenses | $57,092 | $22,596 | $43,733 | $123,421 |

## Use of Columns

It should be clear that NFPs have a lot of flexibility in presenting information in their financial statements. One aspect of this flexibility is to report disaggregated information by using columns in the financial statements. Organizations may use several columns to present information as long as certain totals for the entity are reported. For example, the statement of financial position must report total assets, total liabilities, and total net assets, as well as totals for the three classes of net assets.

Organizations may report columns in the financial statements to convey a variety of information. Some of the approaches used are as follows:

- *Net asset class* – An advantage of reporting the statement of activities in this format is that total contributions for the organization are shown, and the reclassifications between classes of net assets are easy to see. Exhibit 1-2 (shown earlier) is an example of a statement of activities with columns for each class of net assets. Some NFPs also use this format for the statement of financial position.
- *Operating based formats* – Some organizations find it useful to break out operating activities from other activities. For example:
    - *Operating and plant* – Some organizations find it useful to show activities and balances related to land, building, and equipment separate from their operating activities.
    - *Operating and investments* – Some organizations have substantial amounts in endowment and similar types of investments and find it helpful to report this information separately.

- *Fund information* – For some organizations, fund information remains important for external financial reporting. Columns can be used for each fund as long as certain totals for the entity are reported.

Organizations also have the flexibility of different columns among the financial statements. For example, an organization may only have one column in the statement of financial position and use three columns in the statement of activities to report information by net asset class.

The examples we have discussed are just some of the ways an organization may display information in the financial statements. Again, organizations have a significant amount of flexibility in financial statement formats. However, in all cases, organizations must report the basic information that focuses on the entity as a whole.

## KNOWLEDGE CHECK

7.  Which is true of the use of columns?

    a.  Organizations may report columns in the financial statements to convey a variety of information.
    b.  Organizations never find it useful to break out operating activities from other activities.
    c.  Fund information is never important for external financial reporting.
    d.  The statement of activities must report four columns of information.

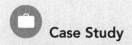

**Case Study**

Case Study Background Information

The New River Performing Arts, Inc. (NRPA) is a private NFP located in the mountains of Virginia. The organization owns a local theater that is an historic landmark. It can hold 400 people. The organization supports the area's symphony and several theatrical performances a year. Ticket prices for both the symphony and theatrical performances do not cover the costs of these productions. NRPA depends on private contributions to cover approximately one-third of the costs of operations.

Recently, NRPA hired Tom Chase as their accountant. Tom is a business graduate of the local community college and has five years of accounting experience with the town of Dublin. He is familiar with fund accounting used by local governments, but is new to the reporting requirements of NFPs. With the help of his accounting textbook from college, Tom has prepared the statement of operations for the year just ended. He used the three classes of net assets described in the book and elected to report the functional classification of expenses on the face of the statement.

On the following page is the statement of operations prepared by Tom.

| New River Performing Arts, Inc. Statement of Operations Year Ended June 30, 201X (in thousands) | | | |
|---|---|---|---|
| | Unrestricted | Temporarily Restricted | Permanently Restricted |
| Operating revenues | | | |
| Symphony activities | | | |
| Box office and tour | $70,500 | | |
| Media and other revenues | 10,502 | | |
| Theatrical presentations | 5,025 | | |
| Interest and dividends | 3,030 | | |
| Other income | 1,208 | | |
| **Total operating revenues** | 90,265 | | |

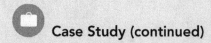

**Case Study (continued)**

### New River Performing Arts, Inc.
### Statement of Operations
### Year Ended June 30, 201X
### (in thousands)

| | Unrestricted | Temporarily Restricted | Permanently Restricted |
|---|---|---|---|
| Operating expenditures | | | |
| Program expenditures | | | |
| Symphony activities | | | |
| Performances | 110,150 | 2,420 | |
| New productions | 5,203 | 3,548 | |
| Other expenditures | 1,414 | | |
| Theatrical presentations | 8,222 | 1,515 | |
| | 124,989 | 7,483 | |
| Supporting services | | | |
| Symphony Hall | 7,556 | | |
| General management | 9,652 | | |
| | 17,208 | - | |
| **Total operating expenditures** | 142,197 | 7,483 | |
| **Loss from operations** | (51,932) | (7,483) | |
| Contributions | $82,452 | | |
| Less: | | | |
| Transfers of restricted gifts | (10,435) | 9,035 | 1,400 |
| Depreciation | (12,517) | | |
| Fund-raising expenditures | (15,005) | | |
| **Other Support and expenditures** | 44,495 | 9,035 | 1,400 |
| **Change in net assets** | (7,437) | 1,552 | 1,400 |
| | | | |
| Net assets | | | |
| Beginning of year | 52,817 | 15,087 | 50,005 |
| End of year | $ 45,380 | $ 16,639 | $ 51,405 |

Case Study Exercise

Please review the statement prepared by Tom. Describe any deficiencies you observe in the statement.

---

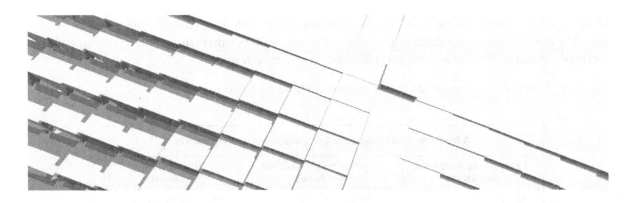

## Chapter 2

# NET ASSET CLASSIFICATIONS

## LEARNING OBJECTIVES

After completing this chapter, you should be able to do the following:

- Differentiate the three classifications of net assets.
- Identify how donor-imposed restriction can be made.

## TECHNICAL BACKGROUND INFORMATION

Not-for-profit entities (NFPs) are unique in that they often receive substantial amounts of contributions. These donations can contain donor-imposed restrictions as to their use. Information about these restrictions on the net resources is important to financial statement users. As illustrated in the following, net assets can be broken down into three classes based on the existence or absence of donor-imposed restrictions.

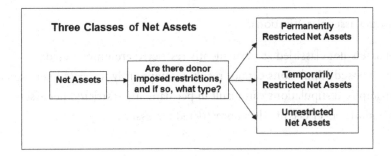

All net assets are classified as unrestricted, unless the net assets result from contributions whose use is limited by donor-imposed stipulations. The stipulations can result in either temporarily or permanently restricted net assets. Without a donor restriction, net assets are unrestricted.

The three classes of net assets are described in more detail in the following diagram:

| A More-Detailed Look at the Three Net Asset Classifications | | |
| --- | --- | --- |
| **Permanently Restricted Net Assets** | **Temporarily Restricted Net Assets** | **Unrestricted Net Assets** |
| The part of the net assets resulting from: <br><br> • Contributions and other inflows of assets whose use by the organization is limited by donor-imposed stipulations that neither expire by passage of time nor can be fulfilled or otherwise removed by actions of the organization. <br><br> • Other asset enhancements and diminishments subject to the same kinds of stipulations. <br><br> • Reclassifications from (or to) other classes of net assets as a consequence of donor-imposed stipulations. | The part of the net assets resulting from: <br><br> • Contributions and other inflows of assets whose use by the organization is limited by donor-imposed stipulations that either expire by the passage of time or can be fulfilled and removed by actions of the organization pursuant to those stipulations. <br><br> • Other asset enhancements and diminishments subject to the same kinds of stipulations. <br><br> • Reclassifications to (or from) other classes of net assets as a consequence of donor-imposed stipulations, their expiration by passage of time or their fulfillment and removal by actions of the organization pursuant to those stipulations. | In the absence of donor-imposed restrictions, all other net assets are classified as unrestricted. A simple way to state this is that all net assets not classified as permanently or temporarily restricted are unrestricted. |

FASB Accounting Standards Update (ASU) 2016-14, *Presentation of Financial Statements of Not-for-Profit Entities*, was released on August 18, 2016. The newly released ASU will change the way all NFPs classify net assets and prepare financial statements. Net assets will be classified as "net assets without donor restrictions" and "net assets with donor restrictions". The standard is effective for annual financial statements issued for fiscal years beginning after December 15, 2017 and for interim periods within fiscal years beginning after December 15, 2018. Early application is permitted. For more information visit www.fasb.org.

## KNOWLEDGE CHECK

1. Which is true of net asset classifications?

    a. All net assets not classified as permanently restricted are unrestricted.

    b. Donor-imposed stipulations cannot result in temporarily restricted net assets.

    c. Donor-imposed stipulations can result in permanently restricted net assets.

    d. Contributions never classified as unrestricted net assets.

Generally, restrictions are stipulated explicitly by the donor in a written or oral communication accompanying the gift. In addition to explicit donor-imposed restrictions, there are certain contributions that may have implied restrictions as follows:

- Restrictions that result implicitly from the circumstances surrounding the receipt of the contributed asset (for example, a contribution received in response to an appeal to raise resources for a new building).
- Contributions of unconditional promises to give with payments due in future periods are inferred to be (therefore are implied to be) and should be reported as temporarily-restricted contributions unless the donor expressly stipulates, or circumstances surrounding the receipt of the promise make clear, that the donor intended it to be used to support activities of the current period.
- Some organizations receive contributions of long-lived assets (for example, equipment and buildings) or cash and other assets restricted to the purchase of long-lived assets. Often, the donor will not expressly stipulate how or how long the long-lived asset must be used by the organization. An organization may adopt one of two policies related to such contributions:
  - *Imply a time restriction on the use of such assets that expires over the assets' expected useful lives.* In such a case, the contribution would be considered temporarily restricted, and the restriction would be met over the asset's expected life via depreciation.
  - *No implied time restriction.* The organization would recognize such gifts of long-lived assets as unrestricted. In addition, the restriction on contributions of cash and other assets for the purchase of such long-lived assets would be met when the long-lived assets are placed into service by the organization.

FASB ASU 2016-14 removes the option to imply a time restriction on the use of such assets that expires over the life of the assets' useful lives. For more information visit www.fasb.org.

## KNOWLEDGE CHECK

2. Which is true of contributions of long-lived assets?

   a. Some organizations receive contributions of long-lived assets or cash and other assets restricted to the purchase of long-lived assets.
   b. The donor will always expressly stipulate how and how long the long-lived asset must be used by the organization.
   c. Contributions of long-lived assets are reported as permanently restricted net assets.
   d. Organization may not imply a time restriction on the use of such assets.

# To Imply or Not to Imply

To illustrate how an accounting policy of implying or not implying time restrictions on contributions of long-lived assets affects net assets, assume that Organizations A and B both receive $200,000 contributions of long-lived assets. The donor did not stipulate how long the assets must be used or how to use any proceeds resulting from the assets' disposal. Also, assume that the assets have a four-year life with no salvage value and that a full year's worth of depreciation was taken in the first year (as the assets were received and placed into service early in the year). Organization A has a policy of implying time restrictions on the use of such contributed assets that expire over the assets' expected useful lives. Organization B does not have a policy of implying time restrictions.

| | Year 1 | Year 2 | Year 3 | Year 4 | Total |
|---|---|---|---|---|---|
| **Organization A – Implied Time Restriction** | | | | | |
| Unrestricted net assets: | | | | | |
|     Net assets released from restrictions | $ 50,000 | 50,000 | 50,000 | 50,000 | $200,000 |
|     Depreciation expense | –50,000 | –50,000 | –50,000 | –50,000 | –200,000 |
| Effect on unrestricted net assets | – | – | – | – | – |
| | | | | | |
| Temporarily restricted net assets: | | | | | |
|     Contributions | $200,000 | – | – | – | $200,000 |
|     Net assets released from restrictions | –50,000 | –50,000 | –50,000 | –50,000 | –200,000 |
| Effect on temporarily restricted net assets | 150,000 | –50,000 | –50,000 | –50,000 | – |
| | | | | | |
| **Organization B – <u>No Implied</u> Time Restriction** | | | | | |
| Unrestricted net assets: | | | | | |
|     Contributions | $200,000 | – | – | – | $200,000 |
|     Depreciation expense | –50,000 | –50,000 | –50,000 | –50,000 | –200,000 |
| Effect on unrestricted net assets | 150,000 | –50,000 | –50,000 | –50,000 | – |

As discussed earlier, temporary restrictions limit the use of assets by donor-imposed stipulations that either expire by passage of time (time restriction) or can be fulfilled and removed by actions of the organization pursuant to those stipulations (purpose restriction). For example, a restriction on a contribution to acquire operating supplies expires when those supplies are acquired by the organization.

In some cases, donor-imposed restrictions are met in the same period that the contribution is received. An organization may adopt an accounting policy that would report such contributions as unrestricted support. For example, suppose a library receives a donation during the year restricted to the purchase of books and expends those resources to purchase books during the same year. The library may adopt a policy to report such contributions as increases in unrestricted net assets. Such a policy would have to be consistent from period to period and properly disclosed in the notes to the financial statements. The organization would also have to have a similar policy for investment gains and income that have donor-imposed restrictions.

## KNOWLEDGE CHECK

3. Which is true of donor-imposed restrictions?

    a. Donor-imposed restrictions are never met in the same period that the contribution is received.
    b. Temporary restrictions limit the use of assets by donor-imposed stipulations that either expire by passage of time or can be fulfilled and removed by actions of the organization pursuant to those stipulations.
    c. Donor-imposed restrictions must be in writing.
    d. Organization must report contribution with donor-imposed restriction that are met in the same period received as unrestricted.

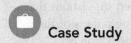 **Case Study**

Dublin College is a private NFP located in the mountains of Virginia. The college enrolls approximately 1,000 students. In addition to tuition, the college depends on contributions to help fund general operations and several specific activities.

The college has adopted the following accounting policies:

- Report contributions with donor-imposed restrictions that are met in the same period that the contribution is received as unrestricted support.
- Imply a time restriction on the use of contributed long-lived assets or of cash restricted to the purchase of long-lived assets that expires over the assets' expected useful lives.

Annual tuition and fees for the college are $32,000 a year. Part of the fees must be used for a future student center. This year $500,000 of the fees was set aside for that purpose.

The college has just finished a fundraising campaign to build a new science building. The college was able to raise $2,500,000 in contributions restricted for the building. In addition, the college issued $1,000,000 in bonds for the building. As part of the bond issue, the college created a debt reserve fund of $100,000. The new science building was completed this year at a cost of $3,000,000. It will be put into service at the beginning of next year.

Every year the college has an annual fund campaign to support the general operations of the college. At year-end, the college had $75,000 of outstanding pledges that will be collected in the next fiscal year. The college expects to collect the full amount.

The college received a $500,000 bequest from the estate of a former art teacher to be used for educational purposes. The Board of Trustees of college voted to create a named endowment for the teacher and use the income to support the art program.

The senior class raised $10,000 as a senior gift to be used for library books. The college purchased $50,000 of library books during the year.

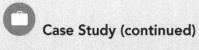

## Case Study (continued)

Case Study Exercise

Review the items listed in the chart below. Indicate the classification that these amounts should be reported under (such as part of unrestricted, temporarily restricted, or permanently restricted net assets) and the reason they belong in that classification. The first one has been done for you.

| Item | Net Asset Classification | Reason... |
|---|---|---|
| The $500,000 of student fees set aside for a future student center | Unrestricted Net Assets | Only a donor can impose a stipulation that makes an amount either temporarily or permanently restricted. This amount is from student fees. Any limitation on the use of assets should be disclosed. This amount can also be reported as a designated amount of unrestricted net assets. |
| The $2,500,000 collected and spent on the new science building | | |
| The $100,000 located in the debt reserve fund | | |
| The $75,000 of outstanding pledges | | |
| The $500,000 received from the bequest | | |
| The $10,000 senior gift | | |

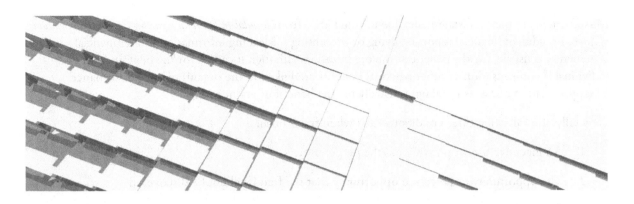

# Chapter 3

# CONSIDERATION OF FRAUD

## LEARNING OBJECTIVES

After completing this chapter, you should be able to do the following:

- Identify the requirements regarding the auditor's consideration of fraud.
- Determine the types of fraud that could exist.
- Identify what risks are presumed to be fraud risks.
- Identify audit procedures to address presumed fraud risks.

## TECHNICAL BACKGROUND INFORMATION

AU-C section 240, *Consideration of Fraud in a Financial Statement Audit*, establishes the requirements for audit procedures and provides application and explanatory information regarding the consideration of fraud. Those requirements address the following topics:

- Professional skepticism
- Discussion among the engagement team
- Risk assessment procedures and related activities
- Identification and assessment of risks of material misstatement due to fraud
- Responses to assessed risks of material misstatement due to fraud
- Evaluation of audit evidence
- Auditor unable to continue the engagement
- Communications to management and those charged with governance
- Communications to regulatory and enforcement authorities
- Documentation

Misstatements in financial statements due to fraud arise from *fraudulent financial reporting* or *misappropriation of assets*. Fraudulent financial reporting (lying or presenting misleading information in the financial statements) is usually for the benefit of the organization, although it can be for the benefit of an individual if compensation or other personal benefits are linked to the organization's performance. Misappropriation of assets (stealing) is usually for the benefit of an individual.

Generally, the following three conditions exist when fraud occurs:

1. An incentive for, or pressure on, the perpetrator

2. The opportunity or perceived opportunity that the fraud will not be discovered

3. Rationalization by the perpetrator or an attitude that justifies the fraud

In a tough economy, pressures to commit fraud can build as household members are laid off, benefits are lost, and unpaid bills multiply. At the same time, opportunities to commit fraud may become available as positions are combined creating heavy workloads or work may be re-assigned to someone not as knowledgeable about the work. An organization's susceptibility to fraud changes as one or more of the three aforementioned conditions change.

It is important for the audit team to exercise professional skepticism, which includes both a questioning mind and a critical assessment of audit evidence. The audit team should conduct the engagement with a mindset that recognizes the possibility that a material misstatement due to fraud could be present regardless of any past experience with the entity and regardless of the audit team's belief about management's honesty and integrity. This may become more challenging when an audit team has worked with an organization for a few years and believes that management is honest and is committed to strong internal control. Members of the audit team may unintentionally lose some of their skepticism.

Audit teams may have a tendency to focus on misappropriation of assets, particularly when financial statements appear straightforward and do not include complex revenue recognition issues. However, even simple not-for-profits can have motivation to misstate their financial statements fraudulently.

| **Fraudulent financial reporting in a not-for-profit entity can include incentives or pressures to do the following:** |
| --- |
| $   Increase the percentage of program services compared to total expenses. |
| $   Minimize fundraising expenses. |
| $   Report restricted gifts as unrestricted. |
| $   Allocate costs to grants inappropriately. |
| $   Recognize revenue belonging to future periods so as not to show a negative change in net assets. |
| $   Make other misclassifications that have tax consequences or affect the organization's exempt status. |

To identify potential pressures or incentives for fraudulent financial reporting, the audit team should consider the following business risks to the organization:

- What percent of program costs (or fundraising costs) are grantors expecting to see?
- What is the effect on future funding for not meeting those expectations?
- What is the effect of the classification of contributions as restricted (temporarily or permanently) versus unrestricted on current liquidity?
- What is the effect on the public support percentage for IRS purposes of the classification of a particular revenue stream?

## KNOWLEDGE CHECK

1. Which is true of fraudulent financial reporting in not-for-profit entities?

    a. Not-for-profits may experience incentives or pressures to increase the percentage of program services compared to total expenses.

    b. Not-for-profits may experience incentives or pressures to increase the percentage of fundraising expenses compared to total expenses.

    c. Not-for-profits never experience incentives or pressures to report restricted gifts as unrestricted.

    d. Not-for-profits may experience pressure to recognize expense belonging to future periods so as not to show a negative change in net assets.

2. Which is typically NOT true of fraudulent financial reporting in not-for-profit entities?

    a. Not-for-profits may experience incentives or pressure to allocate costs to grants inappropriately.

    b. Not-for-profits may experience incentives or pressure for misclassifications to report results similar to for-profit entities for similar programs.

    c. Not-for-profits may experience incentives or pressure to recognize revenue belonging to future periods.

    d. Not-for-profits may experience incentives or pressure for misclassifications that have tax consequences or affect an organization's exempt status.

Auditors obtain information to answer these questions and identify fraud risk factors through the following:

- Inquiries
- Consideration of analytical procedures
- Consideration of other information that may be helpful to identify fraud risks

Because the audit team needs to have some information about the organization to identify fraud risk factors, the audit team will most likely have done some preliminary work before having a meaningful brainstorming session. This work may consist of preliminary inquiries of personnel, performing preliminary analytical procedures, and gaining at least a preliminary understanding of the organization and its internal control.

Inquiries can provide valuable information regarding fraud risk factors. Certainly direct questions are appropriate regarding knowledge of fraud, allegations of fraud, or potential ways fraud could occur in the organization. However, inquiries about controls, co-workers' behavior, accounting "trouble spots," complex adjustments, or allocations can also provide valuable information. Identifying areas that require significant time to reconcile or record transactions may signify a fraud risk factor. Analytical procedures can also provide valuable information regarding fraud risk factors. Procedures that compare actual results to expectations based on an understanding of the industry can at times identify fraud risk factors quickly. The audit team should recognize that analytical procedures that merely compare current results to prior period results will not usually identify an ongoing fraud.

## KNOWLEDGE CHECK

3. Which type of inquiries are the least likely to provide valuable information regarding fraud risk factors?

   a. Inquiries regarding knowledge of fraud.
   b. Inquiries regarding experience with fraud.
   c. Inquiries regarding allegations of fraud.
   d. Inquiries regarding potential ways fraud could occur.

Discussion of fraud risk factors among the audit team should involve the key members of the audit team. It may be helpful to include IT specialists or tax personnel preparing or reviewing the tax return(s) or offering tax advice. They may provide information to the audit team regarding fraud risk factors that should be addressed by audit procedures.

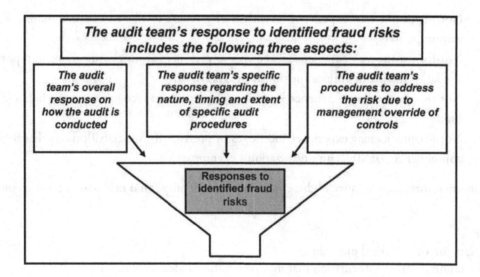

An audit team's overall response on how the audit is conducted includes the assignment of personnel and supervision; the consideration of accounting principles selected and applied by the client; and the predictability of auditing procedures. An audit team's specific response includes the specific audit procedures that will be performed to address identified fraud risk factors. An audit team's response will also include how the audit team addresses specific risks identified in auditing standards.

The identification and evaluation of fraud risk factors is an ongoing process throughout the audit. The audit team should maintain a questioning mind and a critical assessment of audit evidence throughout the audit. This may require adjustment or amendment to the audit plan to address all identified fraud risk factors. The audit team should develop procedures to address identified specific fraud risks. As part of the concluding process to the audit, the audit team should evaluate if all identified fraud risk factors were addressed appropriately.

## KNOWLEDGE CHECK

4. Which is true of fraud risk factors?

   a. The audit team should recognize that analytical procedures which compare current results to prior period results will always identify an ongoing fraud.
   b. Analytical procedures can always provide valuable information regarding fraud risk factors.
   c. Analytical procedures are the best procedures for the auditor to address the risk of material misstatement due to fraud.
   d. Discussion of fraud risk factors among the audit team should always involve the key members of the audit team.

5. Which is true of an audit team's overall response on how the audit is conducted?

   a. The response is not required to include the consideration of the assignment of personnel and supervision.
   b. The response includes the consideration of accounting principles selected and applied by the client.
   c. The response includes the consideration of the number of personnel on the engagement team.
   d. The response on how the audit is conducted includes using standardized, predictable auditing procedures.

| Auditing standards presume that risks of fraud in revenue recognition exist and could include the following: |
| --- |
| $ Improper classification of revenue among the three net asset classes (unrestricted, temporarily restricted, or permanently restricted). |
| $ Recognizing conditional promises to give as unconditional. |
| $ Recognizing intentions to give as promises to give. Recognizing pledges uncollectible through a known insufficient estimate of reserves. |
| $ Agency transactions not recognized as such. |
| $ In-kind contributions recognized inappropriately. |

# KNOWLEDGE CHECK

6. Which is true of improper revenue recognition?

    a. Improper revenue recognition excludes improper classification of revenue among the three net asset classes.

    b. Improper revenue recognition includes recognizing the functional classification of related expenses.

    c. Improper revenue recognition includes recognizing conditional promises to give as unconditional.

    d. Improper revenue recognition excludes recognizing intentions to give as promises to give.

Audit standards also require the auditor to design and perform audit procedures responsive to management override of controls as a fraud risk. Audit procedures that should be performed regarding this consideration include

- testing the appropriateness of journal entries and adjustments;
- review of accounting estimates (for example, allocation of costs, such as general or administrative expenses, between functional classifications) for biases that could result in a material misstatement due to fraud; and
- evaluation of business rationale for significant, unusual transactions.

 **Case Study**

## Case Study Background Information

The following information has been identified by the audit team thus far during preliminary engagement activities.

Struggling NFP provides youth support services for children ages five to 12, including education support, physical development opportunities, and counseling.

Struggling NFP has the following personnel:

- Office manager, who performs the accounting and has been with Struggling NFP for over five years. Your audit firm has a good rapport with the office manager
- Executive director, who has also worked at Struggling NFP for over five years. Your audit firm also has a good rapport with the executive director
- Resource development manager, who started at the end of the previous fiscal year
- Lucy Lou, a program manager, who has been at the organization for just over three years
- Sam Smith, the other program manager, who had been at the organization for almost two years
- Certified counselor, who works as needed based on client needs: The counselor also works for a nearby city school district. The counselor is considered an employee for insurance coverage purposes, based on legal advice.

During the year, Sam Smith was let go due to budget concerns, and his work was moved to Lucy Lou. The office manager's hours were cut to part time.

Struggling NFP receives about 50 percent of its support from individual donations, most of which come from an annual dinner and silent auction. Revenue from the annual dinner was down about 20 percent from the prior year. Struggling NFP receives the other 50 percent of its support from corporate and foundation grants. The grants are for general purposes, and the only requirement is an annual report explaining what the organization accomplished. The organization includes in its report how many clients were served and a spotlight on the story of one client. The reports are prepared by the resource development manager, and the executive director receives copies.

The assets of the organization consist of cash, a small inventory of program supplies (for example, books, athletic equipment, and art supplies), office equipment (for example, computers and a copier), program equipment (such as computers), and office furniture. The liabilities of the organization consist of accounts payable and payroll related liabilities. The significant expenses of the organization are payroll, employee benefits, facility lease, program supplies, office supplies, and insurance. Struggling NFP has no temporarily restricted or permanently restricted net assets.

## ⬛ Case Study (continued)

Supplies are ordered or purchased for reimbursement by the various managers. Invoices are approved by the executive director for payment. Disbursements are made weekly for approved invoices. Rent is the only nonpayroll exception for which the organization receives no invoice. The office manager pays rent for the following month during the last week of the current month. Checks are attached to the supporting documentation when submitted to the executive director for signature. The executive director and the board president are the only authorized personnel to sign checks. The office manager mails payments once the checks have been signed.

Payroll is semi-monthly, and employees are paid the last day of the pay period. Time sheets are turned in the day before the last day of the pay period with estimated hours for the last day. The counselor is the only exception. If she has hours on the last day of the pay period, they are included in the next pay period. If time sheets are for other than four or eight hours per day, inclusive of all time such as for vacation, the office manager has the executive director approve the time sheet. The executive director approves all of the counselor's time sheets. The payroll check register is submitted with payroll checks to the executive director for signature. The executive director distributes payroll checks to the employees.

Dinner tickets are sold by all personnel and board members. Unsold tickets are returned to the resource development manager (RDM). The RDM provides the office manager with a schedule of tickets sold reconciled to funds received on a weekly basis starting two months before the dinner, with increasing frequency within the last two weeks of the event. Items donated for the silent auction are inventoried by the RDM, with every donor receiving a thank you letter listing the item(s) donated. Payment for auction items won must be made at time of the auction. The RDM and one of the program managers accept the checks or complete credit card charge slips for the amounts of the winning bids and then attach them to the bid slip. Some items are paid for with cash, and there are a few cash donations. In both circumstances, the payor receives a receipt for payment. A duplicate receipt is attached to the bid slip, and general donation receipts are put in a separate envelope.

The day after the dinner, the office manager copies the checks and prepares deposits. The office manager likes to have a separate deposit for auction money and general donation money. Either that day or the next, the office manager processes the credit card charges.

Grant funds are received annually or quarterly, depending on the grant. Grant correspondence and copies of checks are provided to the RDM. Contribution revenue is recorded when the organization is notified that the grant is approved, which may be when the grant funds are received or the first quarter funds are received. Deposits are written up by the office manager and taken to the bank by whomever is available to do so.

Bank statements are opened by the executive director. The bank does not return checks or provide copies of checks. However, the executive director does have online access to the bank account and checks the bank balance at least twice a week. If she does not recognize the amount of a check that has cleared, she views the check online. The bank reconciliation is performed by the office manager on a timely basis.

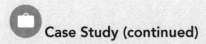 **Case Study (continued)**

Costs are allocated on a functional basis as follows:

- Program services include payroll and related costs for program managers and 90 percent of payroll and related costs for the executive director; 70 percent of the facility lease and property insurance; program supplies; liability insurance; and other direct costs.
- Management and general costs include payroll and related costs for the office manager; half of the payroll and related costs for the resource development manager; 10 percent of the payroll and related costs for the executive director; 30 percent of the facility lease and property insurance; office supplies; errors and omission insurance; and audit fees.
- Fundraising costs include half of the payroll and related costs for the RDM; office supplies and postage directly for the dinner or grant reports; and the cost of the dinner, including facility rental, catering, and more.

Subsequent to year-end, one of the foundations gave notification that it will not be able to provide a grant for the next fiscal year due to the poor performance of the foundation's investments. The executive director laid off the RDM and is currently performing the RDM's tasks.

Case Study Exercise

1. You are part of the audit team for Struggling NFP. What are the fraud risk factors you will identify in the audit team discussion?

2. AU-C section 240 requires the auditor to presume that risks of fraud in revenue recognition exist. What procedures could the audit team perform to address this risk?

3. What procedures could your audit team perform to address the fraud risk of management override of controls?

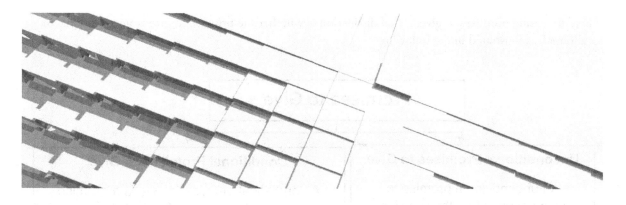

## Chapter 4

# PROMISES TO GIVE

## LEARNING OBJECTIVES

After completing this chapter, you should be able to do the following:

- Identify key concepts related to promises to give.
- Distinguish between conditional and unconditional promises to give.
- Identify intentions to give.

## TECHNICAL BACKGROUND INFORMATION

### Promises to Give

In general terms, a *promise to give* is a written or oral agreement to contribute cash or other assets to another entity. A promise to give may be either conditional or unconditional. The FASB *Accounting Standards Codification* (ASC) glossary offers a more formal definition:

> **Promise to Give**
>
> A promise to give is a written or oral agreement to contribute cash or other assets to another entity. A promise carries rights and obligations. The recipient of a promise to give has a right to expect that the promised assets will be transferred in the future, and the maker has a social and moral obligation, and generally a legal obligation, to make the promised transfer. A promise to give may be either conditional or unconditional.

When discussing promises to give, a vital distinction is whether the promise to give is unconditional or conditional, as illustrated in the following:

| **Promises to Give** |
|---|

| **Unconditional Promises to Give**<br><br>An unconditional promise to give occurs when the promise to give is satisfied only by (a) the passage of time or (b) the demand by the promisee for performance.<br><br>An unconditional promise to give is recognized as revenue when the promise is received. | **Conditional Promises to Give**<br><br>A conditional promise to give is a promise to give where the performance of the promise is dependent upon the occurrence of (a) a specified and (b) a future uncertain event that bind the promisor.<br><br>A conditional promise to give is recognized as revenue upon satisfaction of a qualifying event whereby the promise to give becomes unconditional. |
|---|---|

## KNOWLEDGE CHECK

1.  Which is true of promises to give?

    a.  When discussing promises to give, a vital distinction is whether the promise to give is unconditional or conditional.

    b.  A promise to give must be conditional.

    c.  An unconditional promise to give cannot be recognized when it is received.

    d.  An unconditional promise to give is recognized as revenue when the cash or asset is received.

Not-for-profits may enter into written or oral agreements with donors involving future nonreciprocal transfers of cash, other assets, and services.[1] Such agreements between not-for-profits and potential donors should be reported as contribution revenue and receivables if such agreements are, in substance, unconditional promises to give, even if the promises are not legally enforceable. In recording revenue, it is important to be mindful, especially where promises to give are oral, that recognition eligibility is subject to certain verifiable documentation criteria.

An unconditional promise to give shall be recognized when it is received. However, to be recognized there must be sufficient evidence in the form of verifiable documentation that a promise was made and received. The requirement (that there be sufficient evidence that a promise was made and received) does

---

[1] FASB ASC 958-605 notes, "promises to give services generally involve personal services that, if not explicitly conditional, are often implicitly conditioned upon the future and uncertain availability of specific individuals whose services have been promised."

not preclude recognition of verifiable oral promises, such as those documented by tape recordings, written registers, or other means that permit subsequent verification. Other forms of sufficient verifiable evidence documenting that a promise was made by the donor and received by the not-for-profit include

- written agreements;
- pledge cards;
- oral promises documented by contemporaneous written logs; and
- oral promises documented by follow-up written confirmations.

A conditional promise to give is considered unconditional if the possibility that the condition will not be met is remote.

A transfer of assets with a conditional promise to contribute them shall be accounted for as a refundable advance until the conditions have been substantially met or explicitly waived by the donor. Some entities transfer cash or other assets with both donor-imposed restrictions and stipulations that impose a condition on which a gift depends. If a restriction and a condition exist, the transfer shall be accounted for as a refundable advance until the condition on which it depends is substantially met. A transfer of assets after a conditional promise to give is made and before the conditions are met is the same as a transfer of assets with a conditional promise to contribute those assets. A change in the original conditions of the agreement between promisor and promisee shall not be implied without an explicit waiver.

A communication that does not indicate clearly whether it is a promise is considered an unconditional promise to give if it indicates an unconditional intention to give that is legally enforceable. Legal enforceability refers to the availability of legal remedies, not the intent to use them.

Conditional promises to give cash or other assets (such as securities or property and equipment) should be recognized as contribution revenue and receivables when the conditions on which they depend are substantially met, that is, when the conditional promise becomes unconditional.

Per the FASB ASC 958, *Not-for-Profit Entities*, contributions of unconditional promises to give with payments due in future periods should be reported as restricted support unless explicit donor stipulations or circumstances surrounding the receipt of a promise make clear that the donor intended it to be used to support activities of the current period. It is reasonable to assume that, by specifying future payment dates, donors indicate that their gift is to support activities in each period in which a payment is scheduled. Thus, unconditional promises to give that are due in future periods, and that are not permanently restricted, generally increase temporarily restricted net assets, rather than unrestricted net assets. If, however, the donor explicitly stipulates that the promise to give is to support current-period activities, or, if other circumstances surrounding the promise make it clear that the donor's intention is to support current-period activities, unconditional promises to give should be reported as unrestricted support that increases unrestricted net assets.

Depending on the existence and nature of donor-imposed restrictions, unconditional promises to give should be reported either as unrestricted support that increases unrestricted net assets, or as restricted support that increases permanently restricted or temporarily restricted net assets. Use of the permanently restricted classification is appropriate if donor-imposed restrictions stipulate that the resources must be maintained permanently. Use of the temporarily restricted classification is appropriate if donor-imposed restrictions (*a*) expire by passage of time or (*b*) can be fulfilled or removed by actions of the not-for-profit entity pursuant to donor stipulations.

Promises to give that do not discuss the specific time or place for the contribution, but that are otherwise clearly unconditional in nature, should be considered unconditional promises to give.

## KNOWLEDGE CHECK

2. Which is true of not-for-profits?

    a. Not-for-profits may enter into written agreements with donors involving future nonreciprocal transfers of cash.

    b. Not-for-profits may not enter into written agreements with donors involving future nonreciprocal transfers of assets.

    c. Not-for-profits may not enter into written agreements with donors involving future nonreciprocal transfers of services.

    d. Not-for-profits may not enter into written agreements with donors that are revocable involving future transfer of assets.

3. Which is true of not-for-profits?

    a. Not-for-profits may not enter into oral agreements with donors involving future nonreciprocal transfers of cash.

    b. Not-for-profits may not enter into oral agreements with donors involving future nonreciprocal transfers of assets.

    c. Not-for-profits may enter into oral agreements with donors involving future nonreciprocal transfers of services.

    d. Not-for-profits may not enter into oral donor agreements that are revocable involving future transfer of assets.

### Intentions to Give

Not-for-profits may receive communications that are intentions to give, rather than promises to give. An example is presented in the following illustration.

| Last Will and Testament of A. Nice Guy | **Good Intentions** |
| --- | --- |
| Upon my death, I, A. Nice Guy, having no heirs, desire that my entire estate be given to the Noble Not-for-profit to support its mission. | Communications from individuals indicating that a not-for-profit has been included in an individual's will as a beneficiary are intentions to give. Such communications are not unconditional promises to give, because individuals retain the ability to modify their wills during their lifetimes. When the probate court declares the will valid, the not-for-profit should recognize contribution revenue and a receivable at the fair value of its interest in the estate, unless the promise is conditioned upon future or uncertain events, in which case a contribution should not be recognized until the conditions are substantially met. Not-for-profits should disclose information about conditional promises in valid wills. |

Solicitations for donations that include clear wording such as "information to be used for budget purposes only," or that allow resource providers, clearly and explicitly, to rescind their indications that they will give, are intentions to give rather than promises to give, and should not be reported as contributions.

### A Few Additional Thoughts

Determining whether a promise is conditional or unconditional can be difficult. Some donor stipulations do not state clearly whether the right to receive payment or the delivery of promised assets depends on meeting those stipulations. It may also be difficult to determine whether stipulations are conditions or restrictions. In cases of vague donor stipulations, a promise containing stipulations that are not clearly unconditional will be presumed to be a conditional promise.

The absence of a specified time for transfer of cash or other assets, by itself, does not necessarily lead to a conclusion that a promise to give is ambiguous. If the parties fail to express the time or place of performance, and performance is unconditional, performance within a reasonable time after making a promise is an appropriate expectation. Similarly, if a promise is conditional, performance within a reasonable time after fulfilling the condition is an appropriate expectation. Promises to give that are silent about payment terms but otherwise are clearly unconditional shall be accounted for as unconditional promises to give.

## KNOWLEDGE CHECK

4.  Which is true of intentions to give?

    a.  Not-for-profits may receive communications that are intentions to give, rather than promises to give.
    b.  Solicitations for donations that clearly include wording such as "information to be used for budget purposes only" should be reported as contributions.
    c.  Solicitations for donations that clearly and explicitly allow resource providers to rescind their indications that they will give should be reported as contributions.
    d.  Intentions to give are always recorded when the intention is given to the not-for-profits.

5.  Which is true of promises to give?

    a.  Promises to give that are silent about payment terms but otherwise are clearly unconditional shall be accounted for as unconditional promises to give.
    b.  All donor stipulations state clearly whether the right to receive payment or the delivery of promised assets depends on meeting those stipulations.
    c.  The absence of a specified time for transfer of cash or other assets, by itself, leads to a conclusion that a promise to give is ambiguous.
    d.  Promises to give are like intentions to give and should not be recognized until the cash or asset is received.

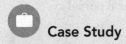

## Case Study

Review the items listed in the following chart related to a capital campaign. Indicate whether the promises received are conditional or unconditional and when the promises should be recorded.

| Situation | Is the promise to give conditional or unconditional? | When would you record the promise to give? |
|---|---|---|
| The executive director of College A approaches Sam Jones and discusses the potential construction of a new athletic building on the campus. The projected costs are $10,000,000 per the architect's plans and estimates. Sam Jones is an alumnus of the college and was an All-American hockey player who also played professional hockey. The building will include a hockey arena, basketball complex, and other indoor sports. Sam Jones indicates he will commit $500,000 provided the building campaign raises the necessary funds to complete construction. | | |
| The executive director of College A approaches the Wagner Foundation, which was formed by a former graduate who retired as a partner from a Big 4 CPA firm. This foundation makes grants to local charities from its investment earnings each year. He indicates "If the foundation will commit $500,000 to the campaign, we will place the graduate's name on the cornerstone of the building as a platinum contributor." The foundation sends the college a commitment letter for the $500,000, "provided the college does place Mr. Wagner's name on the cornerstone of the building as a platinum contributor." | | |
| The executive director of College A now approaches another graduate who has substantial business interests. Mr. Smith has contributed to the college in the past. He tells Mr. Smith that he has raised approximately $3,000,000 of the $10,000,000 needed to construct the building. Mr. Smith indicates he needs to think about it. | | |

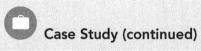 **Case Study (continued)**

| Situation | Is the promise to give conditional or unconditional? | When would you record the promise to give? |
| --- | --- | --- |
| A week later, Mr. Smith sends a letter to College A indicating that he could commit $100,000 a year for the next five years "provided you name the facility the H.G. Smith Athletic Building." | | |
| Later in the campaign, the executive director of College A now has commitments totaling $8,000,000 from various entities. He approaches Widget Makers, Inc., a large international company in the area that is privately owned by two families. All the family members have attended and graduated from College A. As he talks to the CEO and president of the board, Mr. Gotcha and Mr. Now, they indicate that they would be willing to commit the remaining $2,000,000 provided the College names the facility the "Widget Makers Athletic Complex." The executive director indicates that he has a commitment of $500,000 from another graduate that wants the building named after him. Mr. Gotcha and Mr. Now both laugh and say simultaneously, "We will then commit $2,500,000!" | | |

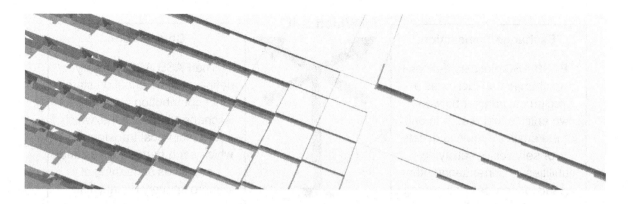

## Chapter 5

# DISTINGUISHING CONTRIBUTIONS FROM EXCHANGE TRANSACTIONS

## LEARNING OBJECTIVES

After completing this chapter, you should be able to do the following:

- Analyze the thought process used to distinguish contributions from exchange transactions.
- Distinguish the accounting differences between contribution and exchange transaction revenues.
- Identify indicators useful in distinguishing contributions from exchange transactions.

## TECHNICAL BACKGROUND INFORMATION

Not-for-profits receive inflows of resources from others to support their missions. This sounds simple enough, but it often is not. Different resource inflows have different accounting and reporting requirements. In some situations, it is difficult to distinguish one type of resource inflow from another. A common area of consternation is trying to distinguish contributions from exchange transactions.

**Which is it?**

| Exchange Transaction | Contribution |
|---|---|
| FASB ASC glossary defines exchange transaction as a reciprocal transfer between two entities that results in one of the entities acquiring assets or services or satisfying liabilities by surrendering other assets or services or incurring other obligations. | The FASB ASC glossary definition of contribution states that contributions differ from exchange transactions, which are reciprocal transfers in which each party receives and sacrifices something of approximately equal value. |

In some situations, exchange transactions can be distinguished easily from contributions, but in other cases, the determination is not as clear-cut.

### The Exercise of Judgment

Classifying asset transfers as exchange transactions or as contributions may require the exercise of judgment concerning whether a reciprocal transaction has occurred; that is, whether a recipient not-for-profit has given up assets, rights or privileges approximately equal to the value of the assets, rights, or privileges received. Value should be assessed from both the recipient not-for-profit's and the resource provider's points of view, and can be affected by a wide variety of factors.

The following illustration, derived from the AICPA *Not-for-Profit Entities Audit & Accounting Guide*, contains the list of indicators from the FASB *Accounting Standards Codification* (ASC) 958, *Not-for-Profit Entities*, that may be helpful in determining whether individual asset transfers are contributions, exchange transactions, or a combination of both.

| Indicators Useful in Distinguishing Contributions From Exchange Transactions | | |
|---|---|---|
| **Indicator** | **Contribution** | **Exchange Transaction** |
| Recipient not-for-profit's intent in soliciting the asset* | Recipient not-for-profit asserts that it is soliciting the asset as a contribution | Recipient not-for-profit asserts that it is seeking resources in exchange for specified benefits |
| Resource provider's expressed intent about the purpose of the asset to be provided by recipient not-for-profit | Resource provider asserts that it is making a donation to support the not-for-profit's programs | Resource provider asserts that it is transferring resources in exchange for specified benefits |

| | Indicators Useful in Distinguishing Contributions From Exchange Transactions | |
| --- | --- | --- |
| **Indicator** | **Contribution** | **Exchange Transaction** |
| Method of delivery | The time or place of delivery of the asset to be provided by the recipient not-for-profit to third-party recipients is at the discretion of the not-for-profit | The method of delivery of the asset to be provided by the recipient not-for-profit to third-party recipients is specified by the resource provider |
| Method of determining amount of payment | The resource provider determines the amount of the payment | Payment by the resource provider equals the value of the assets to be provided by the recipient not-for-profit, or the assets' cost plus markup; the total payment is based on the quantity of assets to be provided |
| Penalties assessed if not-for-profit fails to make timely delivery of assets | Penalties are limited to the delivery of assets already produced and the return of the unspent amount (The not-for-profit is not penalized for nonperformance) | Provisions for economic penalties exist beyond the amount of payment (The not-for-profit is penalized for nonperformance) |
| Delivery of assets to be provided by the recipient not-for-profit | Assets are to be delivered to individuals or organizations other than the resource provider | Assets are to be delivered to the resource provider or to individuals or organizations closely connected to the resource provider |

*This table refers to assets. Assets may include services. The terms *assets* and *services* are used interchangeably in this table.

## KNOWLEDGE CHECK

1.  Which is true of indicators that are useful in distinguishing contributions from exchange transactions?

    a.  Useful indicators include the method of determining the amount of payment.
    b.  Useful indicators exclude the penalties assessed if the not-for-profit fails to make timely delivery of assets.
    c.  Useful indicators exclude the delivery of assets to be provided by the recipient not-for-profit.
    d.  Useful indicators include when the auditor agrees with the client.

2. Which is true of indicators that are useful in distinguishing contributions from exchange transactions?

   a. The time or place of delivery of the asset to be provided by the recipient not-for-profit to third-party recipients being at the discretion of the not-for-profit is indicative of a contribution.

   b. The method of delivery of the asset to be provided by the recipient not-for-profit to third-party recipients being specified by the resource provider is indicative of a contribution.

   c. The resource provider determining the amount of the payment is indicative of an exchange transaction.

   d. The recipient's intent in soliciting the asset over-rides the intent of the resource provider.

3. Which is true of indicators that are useful in distinguishing contributions from exchange transactions?

   a. The not-for-profit not being penalized for nonperformance is indicative of a contribution.

   b. The not-for-profit being penalized for nonperformance is indicative of a contribution.

   c. Assets being delivered to individuals or organizations other than the resource provider are indicative of an exchange transaction.

   d. The recipient's intent in soliciting the asset over-rides the intent of the resource provider.

Depending on the facts and circumstances, some indicators may be more significant than others; however, no single indicator is determinative of the classification of a particular transaction. Indicators of a contribution tend to describe transactions in which the value, if any, returned to the resource provider is incidental to potential public benefits. Indicators of an exchange tend to describe transactions in which the potential public benefits are secondary to the potential proprietary benefits to the resource provider.

Voluntary asset transfers that may be difficult to classify could include:

- **_Membership dues_** – These transfers often have elements of both a contribution and an exchange transaction because members receive tangible or intangible benefits from their membership in the not-for-profit. Usually, the determination of whether membership dues are contributions rests on whether the value received by the member is commensurate with the dues paid. For example, if a not-for-profit has annual dues of $100 and the only benefit members receive is a monthly newsletter with a fair value of $25, $25 of the dues are received in an exchange transaction and should be recognized as revenue as the earnings process is completed and $75 of the dues are a contribution.

- **_Grants, awards, or sponsorships_** – FASB ASC 958-605 discusses transactions in which foundations, business organizations, and other types of entities provide resources to not-for-profits under programs referred to as grants, awards, or sponsorships. A grant or sponsorship may be entirely a contribution, entirely an exchange transaction, or a combination of the two. In addition, those transactions may also have characteristics of agency transactions. Those asset transfers are contributions if the resource providers receive no value in exchange for the assets transferred, or if the value received by the resource providers is incidental to the potential public benefit from using the assets transferred. A grant made by a resource provider to a not-for-profit would likely be a contribution if the activity specified by the grant is to be planned and carried out by the not-for-profit and the not-for-profit has the right to the benefits of carrying out the activity. If, however, the grant is made by a resource provider that provides materials to be tested in the activity, and that provider retains the right to any patents or other results of the activity, the grant would likely be an exchange transaction.

Some transfers of assets between not-for-profits and governments (such as the sale of goods and services) are exchange transactions. Other transfers of assets between not-for-profits and governments (such as unrestricted support given by state and local governments) are contributions. Other kinds of government transfers (sometimes referred to as grants, awards, or appropriations) have unique characteristics that may make it difficult to determine whether they are contributions or exchange transactions.

FASB ASC 958-605 states that resources received in exchange transactions should be classified as unrestricted revenues and net assets, even in circumstances in which resource providers place limitations on the use of the resources. For example, resources received from governments in exchange transactions in which those governments have placed limitations on the use of the resources should be reported as unrestricted revenues and net assets, because those limitations are not donor-imposed restrictions on contributions.

## KNOWLEDGE CHECK

4.  Which is true of voluntary asset transfers?

    a.  FASB ASC 958-605 discusses transactions in which foundations, business organizations, and other types of entities provide resources to not-for-profits under programs referred to as grants, awards, or sponsorships.
    b.  If a not-for-profit has annual dues of $100 and the only benefit members receive is a monthly newsletter with a fair value of $25, $100 of the dues represents a contribution.
    c.  The determination of whether membership dues are contributions never rests on whether the value received by the member is commensurate with the dues paid.
    d.  Usually, the determination of whether membership dues are contributions does not rests on whether any value received by the member is commensurate with the dues paid.

### Premiums

FASB ASC 958-720 discusses the cost of premiums and whether premiums are given in exchange for resources provided. The cost of premiums (such as postcards or calendars) given to potential donors as part of mass fundraising appeals is a fundraising expense, and the classification of the donations received from the appeal as contributions is unaffected by the fact that premiums were given to potential donors. The premiums are not provided to potential donors in exchange for the assets contributed; they can be kept by all those from whom funds are solicited, regardless of whether a contribution is made. The cost of premiums (such as coffee mugs) that are given to resource providers to acknowledge receipt of a contribution also should be reported as fundraising expenses if those costs are nominal in value compared with the value of the goods or services donated by the resource provider. For example, a not-for-profit may provide a coffee mug to people making a contribution of $50 or more; the mug costs the not-for-profit $1. The not-for-profit should recognize contributions for the total amount contributed and fundraising expense of $1 for each mug provided to donors. The cost of premiums that are greater than nominal in value should be reported as cost of sales.

When a donor receives premiums that are greater than nominal in value in connection with a transaction, the transaction generally should be reported as part exchange transaction and part contribution.

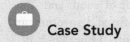

## Case Study

### Case Study Background Information

The Noble Not-for-Profit has a fiscal year ending December 31. Its board of directors wants to provide a free after-school program for children in kindergarten through sixth grade who live in the county in which the not-for-profit is based and whose working parent(s) cannot be home or cannot pick up the children after school. The board has committed approximately $200,000 from unrestricted funds for next year's program, which will be the first year the Noble Not-for-Profit will run the program, and has told the staff to find the additional funding of $600,000 from other sources. The staff projects that it will cost $800,000 in the first year to get the program up and running.

The staff approaches a local foundation and asks if it would be willing to entertain a proposal to fund the project. The executive director of the foundation indicates that the Noble Not-for-Profit will have to put together a grant proposal with the following information:

- Description of the program's operations, goals, and benefits to the community;
- Eligibility criteria for households to receive the care with no charge;
- Copy of the previous year's audited financial statements;
- Budget (by natural classification) of costs to operate the program; and
- Proof of Noble's not-for-profit status from the Internal Revenue Service.

The executive director of the local foundation indicates that the foundation will approve grant proposals in May, with July 1 being the commitment date for the awards made.

After the grant package is completed and submitted in April, the Noble Not-for-Profit receives a grant award letter dated May 15 for $600,000 effective for the period from July 1 through June 30.

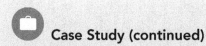 **Case Study (continued)**

Case Study Exercise

1. Is the grant from the local foundation a contribution or an exchange transaction? Please include your rationale for classifying it one way or the other.

2. Based on your answer to the first question, how would Noble Not-for-Profit record the following events?

   ▪ The receipt of the grant award letter from the local foundation on May 15.

   ▪ The first advance of $50,000 foundation funds on July 15.

   ▪ Total program expenses from July 1 through 31$^{st}$ were $70,000. What reclassification of net asset amounts would be recorded on July 31?

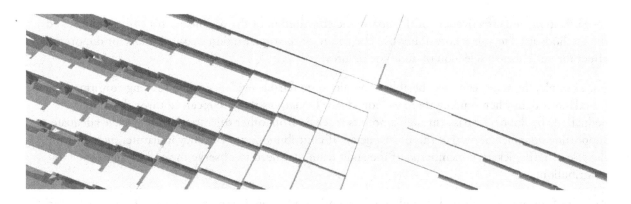

## Chapter 6

# AUDITING CONTRIBUTIONS

## LEARNING OBJECTIVES

After completing this chapter, you should be able to do the following:

- Identify critical concepts involved in auditing contributions.
- Identify the purpose of audit plans and how they are developed.
- Identify how the auditor's understanding of the client and its internal control affects the audit plan.
- Identify how the auditor's assessment of the risk of material misstatement affects the audit plan.
- Identify how to develop audit procedures to obtain sufficient, appropriate evidential matter to support contribution revenue.

## TECHNICAL BACKGROUND INFORMATION

Audit plans detail the procedures an audit team will perform to obtain sufficient, appropriate evidence regarding a particular account balance or class of transactions. Although audit plans need to be comprehensive to allow the owner or audit partner to sign an audit opinion, audit plans also need to be efficient so that the audit firm's resources are well managed. Audit plans are not the starting place, however. Audit plans are the result of other activities and procedures performed by the audit team. Let us look at how we get to the place of developing audit plans.

The audit team, the owner, or audit partner will perform preliminary engagement activities (client acceptance, engagement acceptance, ethical considerations, use of specialists and establishing an understanding with the client). The audit team then gains an understanding of the entity and its environment. This includes, among other factors, its mission, its revenue stream(s), and its donors. During this process, the audit team will identify the users of the financial statements; the involvement, sophistication, and effectiveness of the board; the constitution of the organization's contributions; and the methods used to solicit contributions. The nature of the organization's contributions or donors will affect the audit team's selection of audit procedures.

For example, the audit team may be able to obtain more reliable evidence when sending confirmations to foundations than when sending them to individuals. Donations that are received through payroll deductions by donors or pass-through amounts received from other organizations may have adequate supporting documentation that can be inspected. If contributions are currency in nature, such as from the sale of raffle tickets, a member(s) of the audit team may need to observe the collection of the contributions.

As part of the audit team's understanding of the entity and its environment, the audit team will gain an understanding of the organization's internal control over financial reporting. This includes understanding the organization's control environment or "tone at the top," the organization's process to identify business risks and how they address them, how the organization disseminates information and communicates to those both outside and inside the organization, the procedures or control activities the organization has in place to ensure its processes are being followed, and how the organization monitors its control activities to ensure they are being performed.

Based on the audit team's understanding of the organization and its internal control, the audit team will consider what could go wrong in the processing and recording of transactions. That is, what could happen to materially misstate the financial statements? As part of this consideration, the audit team looks at both misstatements due to error and misstatements due to fraud. This consideration will evaluate each account balance (for example, cash, accounts receivable, accounts payable and more) and each class of transactions (for example, revenue, payroll, other expenses, and more). During this process, the audit team may determine that there is additional information about the entity or its internal control that the audit team should gather. The audit is an evolving process and often revisits previous understandings or considerations as is beneficial to the audit process.

## KNOWLEDGE CHECK

1. Which is NOT true of the audit team gaining an understanding of the organization's internal control?

    a. The audit team should gain an understanding of the organization's control environment or tone at the top.
    b. The audit team should gain an understanding the organization's process to identify business risks and how they address them.
    c. The audit team should gain an understanding of the organization's internal control over operations.
    d. The audit team should gain an understanding how the organization disseminates information or communicates to those both outside and inside the organization.

For each account balance, the audit team will determine the relevant assertions (existence, completeness, valuation, and rights and obligations) and the risk of material misstatement associated with each. For example, if the organization does not deal with foreign currency, the audit team may determine risk of material misstatement for the valuation assertion for cash is negligible.

The audit team also will determine the risk of material misstatement associated with each relevant assertion for each class of transactions (occurrence, completeness, accuracy, cutoff, and classification). It is important to remember that risks will change depending on the assertion. For example, the risk of completeness for payroll transactions may be low (employees can be great reviewers of their paychecks to mitigate understatement). However, the risk of completeness for other cash disbursements may be high or moderate.

Often it is helpful to evaluate account balances with related classes of transactions. For example, if completeness of accounts payable has been determined to be a high risk of material misstatement, then completeness of expenses is likely also to be a high risk of material misstatement. If cutoff of revenue has been determined to be a high risk of material misstatement, it is likely the risk will affect receivables.

## KNOWLEDGE CHECK

2. For each account balance, the audit team will determine the relevant assertions and the risk of material misstatement associated with each. Which is true of this process?

    a. Existence, completeness, and relevance are all assertions related to account balances that the audit team should consider.

    b. Occurrence, classification, and understandability are all assertions related to account balances that the audit team should consider.

    c. Valuation, and rights and obligations are all assertions related to account balances that the audit team should consider.

    d. Classification and reliability are assertions related to account balances that the audit team should consider.

Audit risk, or the risk of material misstatement to the financial statements, is a function of fraud risk, the inherent nature of the account balance or class of transactions, the client's internal controls failing to operate effectively to mitigate misstatements for a particular account balance or class of transactions and detection risk should the audit team not uncover a material misstatement.

Once the audit team has determined the risk(s) of material misstatement by account balance or class of transactions or by assertion, the audit team can determine which audit procedures to perform to obtain sufficient, appropriate evidence for a particular account balance or class of transactions. The audit procedures should directly address the risks identified. For example, if valuation has been identified as a high risk of material misstatement for pledge receivables, the audit team should focus on audit procedures that will provide sufficient, appropriate evidence regarding the valuation of pledge receivables. The audit team may determine that review of subsequent collection of pledges (to the entity's fiscal year-end) will provide the most appropriate evidence regarding valuation. If the audit team has determined that classification of expenses by function (program services, general and management and fundraising) is a high risk, the audit team should develop audit procedures to address this risk.

## KNOWLEDGE CHECK

3. The audit team will determine the risk of material misstatement associated with each relevant assertion for each class of transactions. Which is NOT true of this process?

   a. The audit team should consider timeliness as an assertion related to each class of transactions.
   b. The audit team should consider cut-off as an assertion related to each class of transactions.
   c. The audit team should consider completeness as an assertion related to each class of transactions.
   d. The audit team should consider allocation as an assertion related to each class of transactions.

The following table illustrates an overview of the risk assessment process.

| Overview of the Risk Assessment Process | | |
| --- | --- | --- |
| **Gathering** | **Assessing** | **Responding** |
| The auditor should gather information to obtain an understanding of the auditee and its environment, including its internal control to be able to assess the risks of material misstatement at the financial statement and relevant assertion levels. The auditor should gather this information through risk assessment procedures (for example, inquiries, analytical procedures, and observation and inspection), audit team brainstorming, consideration of fraud risk factors and other means.<br><br>**Note.** The auditor's understanding of internal controls should be sufficient to evaluate the design of controls and determine whether they are implemented and/or operating effectively. | The auditor should then identify and assess the risks of material misstatement at the financial statement and relevant assertion levels related to account balances/class of transactions and disclosures. | To address risks at the overall financial statement level, the auditor should determine overall responses and should design and perform further audit procedures whose nature, timing and extent are responsive to the assessed risks of material misstatement at the relevant assertion levels. |

It is important to design audit plans to obtain sufficient, appropriate evidence. Sufficient evidence refers to the adequacy of the quantity of evidence. Appropriate evidence refers to the quality of evidence. To expend energy to obtain evidence that is not reliable has a detrimental effect on the audit team's efficiency. When sufficient evidence has been obtained to support the audit opinion, acquiring more evidence can also have a detrimental effect on the audit team's efficiency. The audit team should consider both the quantity and the quality of the evidence obtained.

AU-C section 315, *Understanding the Entity and its Environment and Assessing the Risks of Material Misstatements*, and AU-C section 330, *Performing Audit Procedures in Response to Assessed Risks and Evaluating the Audit Evidence Obtained*, establishes the requirements and provides application and explanatory information for the auditor.

It should be noted that pledge receivables do not fit the definition of accounts receivable. The auditor may determine that confirmation of pledges receivable, or the confirmation of specific pledges receivable, will provide sufficient, appropriate evidence. The auditor may also perform other procedures in addition to, or instead of, confirmation of specific pledge receivables to obtain sufficient appropriate evidence. AU-C section 505, *External Confirmations*, establishes requirements for audit procedures and provides application and explanatory information regarding external confirmations.

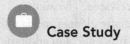

**Case Study**

The following information has been identified thus far in the audit.

Help for Women is a not-for-profit entity providing counseling services to homeless women, connecting them with resources so they may obtain housing and employment or job training services. The organization was founded five years ago and consists of an executive director, an office manager, a part-time bookkeeper, and five counselors.

The organization is supported by contributions from the public. With the recent tough economy, the number of women applying for services has increased. There has been a slight decrease in donations, but the supporters of Help for Women are loyal to its mission and want to support it. The organization typically has had three months of operating expenses in their savings account, but this year that amount has fallen to one month. The organization solicits contributions in the following two ways:

- Board members visit at least two businesses annually asking their employees for contributions. The organization uses National Giving's program of donations through payroll deductions, whereby National Giving collects the payroll deductions and submits the contributions to Help for Women via direct deposit on a monthly basis. Employees sign up for payroll deductions to be made for twelve months at a time.
- The organization has an annual fundraising dinner and solicits pledges for one year, three years, and five years, with donations to be made monthly, quarterly, or annually. There are also significant cash donations received at the dinner.

The board is very active and financially astute, consisting of women executives in the area. The board meets monthly and reviews the financial statements the bookkeeper prints from a well-known accounting software package. The board focuses on the current cash balance and pledges past due. The board also takes time once a quarter to evaluate pledges obtained that are due in each of the next two years so they can plan the organization's expenses and evaluate the organization's future viability.

The bookkeeper is retired from working as a controller of a large not-for-profit for twenty-five years. She wanted work to supplement her retirement income. Although she is not a CPA, she is very knowledgeable about GAAP, particularly as it relates to not-for-profit entities; and, during the time she worked as a controller, she attended AICPA CPE courses relating to not-for-profit accounting.

When a board member visits a business to solicit contributions from its employees, the board member explains that the contributions would support the general activities of the organization and describes the programs of the organization. Employees wanting to contribute are asked to sign a National Giving form that identifies the amount of deduction per paycheck. The business then completes a form identifying the total amount of deductions from its employees and the frequency of payroll. The forms are supplied by National Giving and are in four-part—with the employee, the business, National Giving, and Help for Women each receiving a copy of the form. The forms have a statement in bold print that contributions are for the general use of the organization.

**Case Study (continued)**

At the annual fundraising dinner, pledge forms are provided to each attendee along with an envelope. Attendees are asked to place the pledge form in the envelope and seal them. Any cash donations (via check or currency) are also to be placed in the envelope. Envelopes are collected from each table by board members. The board members then count the envelopes received as a group. The executive director is always anxious to hear the number of envelopes received and finds out as soon as the board members finish counting. A board member delivers the envelopes to the bookkeeper the next day, who opens the envelopes with the office manager. The executive director wants to know how much support they received so she pops in frequently to check their status. The bookkeeper and office manager number each envelope and note the contents of each envelope (pledge form, cash, check, or both) and the name and address of the donor. Sometimes there will just be a $20 bill in the envelope, but usually the cash contributions have the form completed so the organization can send a receipt to the donor. The information is totaled and provided to the board so they can check against the number of total envelopes they received.

The audit team has not identified any significant bias to overstate or understate contribution revenue. The audit team has noted that in situations in which management is uncertain as to which period revenue belongs to, they follow a cash-basis approach and recognize the revenue when the funds are received. The audit team has noticed that in management's (and the board's) optimism, they may have a bias regarding overstatement of receivables. The bookkeeper tends to have a more realistic view of what will be collectible.

Selective financial information listed as follows:

| | |
|---|---|
| Cash | $ 45,000 |
| Pledge receivables – current | $ 205,000 |
| Valuation allowance – current | 0 |
| Pledge receivables – long-term | $ 410,000 |
| Valuation allowance | (10,000) |
| Total assets (including items not previously listed) | $ 700,000 |
| | |
| Contributions – payroll deductions | $ 75,000 |
| Contributions – dinner, one-time gifts | $ 95,000 |
| Contributions – dinner, pledges | $ 255,000 |
| Contributions – as reported on the Statement of Activities | $ 425,000 |
| | |
| Ticket sales – fundraising dinner | $ 12,500 |

**Case Study (continued)**

### Contribution Revenues

The audit team has identified some of the significant risks of material misstatement for *revenues* given the preceding facts as: (1) contribution revenues – payroll deductions; (2) contribution revenues – dinner, one-time gifts; and (3) contribution revenues – dinner, pledges. The audit team then determined the relevant assertions and the risk of material misstatement associated with each of the preceding revenues illustrated as follows:

| Contribution Revenues – Payroll Deductions | | |
| --- | --- | --- |
| **Relevant Assertion by Class of Transaction** | **Factors Considered** | **RMM** |
| Occurrence | Transactions are supported by forms completed by employees and provided to and processed by employer businesses, and contributions withheld are received by National Giving. | Moderate to low |
| Completeness | Organization is aware of businesses visited by board members and is in possession of all paperwork processed during the visit. | Moderate to low |
| Accuracy | Amounts withheld from employees, received by National Giving and contributed to Help for Women are supported by forms completed by employees and processed by businesses, and any discrepancy would be readily addressed within the first month of collection. | Moderate to low |
| Cutoff | Revenue is recorded in the correct period considering the matching principal and timing of processes (such as process cycle time from the date of an employee's payroll deduction to the date of the Help for Women's receipt of the donation). For example, an employee deduction is withheld yearlong bimonthly on the 15th and last day of each month. Typically, the cycle time from deduction to the not-for-profit's receipt follows a 5-day lag. In this example, Help for Women should recognize, in the financial statements of the current period, donation revenue for employee deductions withheld by National Giving on the last day of each month, including the last day of the entity's fiscal year. | High to moderate |

**Case Study (continued)**

| Contribution Revenues – Dinner, One-Time Gifts | | |
|---|---|---|
| **Relevant Assertion by Class of Transaction** | **Factors Considered** | **RMM** |
| Classification | Contributions received are unrestricted as clearly identified by the words "for general use" on the form. | Moderate to low |
| Occurrence | Transactions are supported by deposit of currency or checks. | Moderate to low |
| Completeness | Envelopes are numbered and accounted for by the board as a group, and the contents are viewed together by both the bookkeeper and office manager. | Moderate to low |
| Accuracy | Bank deposits agree to amounts supported by the envelop contents t of currency to checks, as viewed together by the bookkeeper and office manager. | Moderate to low |
| Cutoff | Revenue is recorded in the correct period as supported by the donor contribution receipt date. For example, a donor one-time contribution check received May 25th, at the annual dinner held May 25th, should recognize revenue in the May period, whether the check is deposited in the bank during May, or subsequently, during the month of June. | Moderate to low |
| Classification | Contributions received from the dinner are properly identified as unrestricted, temporarily restricted, or permanently restricted, dependent upon [any, if any] donor designations, such as a memo on a check, which can affect classification (example, a donor may elect to make a contribution exclusively for the acquisition of computer equipment or construction of a child daycare facility). | Moderate to low |

**Case Study (continued)**

| Contribution Revenues –Dinner, Pledges | | |
|---|---|---|
| **Relevant Assertion by Class of Transaction** | **Factors Considered** | **RMM** |
| Occurrence | Envelopes are numbered and accounted for by board as a group, and the contents are accounted for by both the bookkeeper and office manager. | Moderate to low |
| Completeness | Envelopes are numbered and accounted for by the board as a group, and the contents are viewed together by both the bookkeeper and office manager. | Moderate to low |
| Accuracy | Pledges extending beyond one year are to be discounted (reported at net present value). | High to moderate |
| Cutoff | Pledges can be for one, three, or five years, with payments to be made monthly, quarterly, or annually. Revenue should be recorded in the correct period considering the matching principal (regardless of the timing of receipts) consistent with the pledge donation card signed by the donator. Pledge revenues should be recognized in the current period accordingly to an amortization schedule based on [aggregate] pledge revenues over the entire term of the pledge donation. For example, a donor signed pledge card pledging a $5,000 aggregate donation over a five year period should be recognized in the financial statements as $83.34 per month in revenue (60 months x $83.34 = $5,000). | High |
| Classification | The organization does not solicit contributions for specific purposes, however a donor could always write one on the pledge form. | Moderate to low |

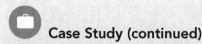

## Case Study (continued)

As discussed in the technical background information, once the audit team has determined the risks of material misstatement, by account balance or class of transactions, by assertion, the audit team can determine which audit procedures to perform to obtain sufficient, appropriate evidence for a particular account balance or class of transactions. The audit procedures should directly address the risks identified. Using the analysis performed by the audit team, develop audit procedures using the following form to address contribution revenue.

### Sample Audit Plan for Contribution Revenue

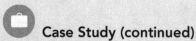 **Case Study (continued)**

Pledges Receivable

The audit team also determined the relevant assertions and the risk of material misstatement associated with pledges receivable illustrated as follows:

| | Pledges Receivable | |
|---|---|---|
| **Relevant Assertion by Class of Transaction** | **Factors Considered** | **RMM** |
| Existence | Pledges are supported by signed pledge forms, the collection and recording of which is processed by more than one individual. Existence can be tested by the auditor using the concept of vouching, whereby transaction selections identified from the financial statements look backwards to signed pledge donation cards to support the existence of the receivable recorded. | Moderate to low |
| Completeness | Pledges are supported by signed pledge forms the, collection and recording of which is processed by more than one individual. Completeness can be tested by the auditor using the concept of tracing, whereby sample pledge donation cards selected by the auditor look forwards to the financial statements to ensure the transaction has been included in the financial statements. | Moderate to low |
| Valuation | Three and five year pledges represent a greater risk of uncollectibility as the donor's circumstances could change, particularly considering the current economic climate. Therefore, the valuation allowance may not appear appropriate, and the auditor may consider an adjustment to more accurately estimate uncollectible pledges. | High |
| Rights and Obligations | There are no apparent restrictions on the organization's right to the pledge receivables and no apparent donor restriction obligations. | Moderate to low |

## Case Study (continued)

Using the analysis performed by the previous audit team, develop audit procedures using the following form to address pledges receivable.

| Sample Audit Plan for Pledges Receivable |
|---|
|  |
|  |
|  |
|  |
|  |
|  |

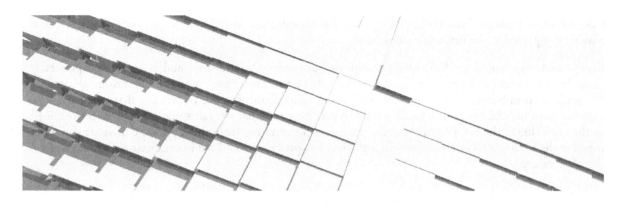

Chapter 7

# CONTRIBUTED SERVICES

## LEARNING OBJECTIVES

After completing this chapter, you should be able to do the following:

- Identify the criteria when contributed services should be recorded and disclosed.
- Determine how contributed services should be recorded.

## TECHNICAL BACKGROUND INFORMATION

Many not-for-profit entities depend on volunteers for a variety of functions. Some contributed services should be recognized in the financial statements as illustrated in the following:

Contributed services should be reported as contribution revenue and as assets or expenses only if

- the services create or enhance a nonfinancial asset (for example, a building), or
- all three of the following apply:
    - The services require specialized skills. (Some examples of specialized skills are accounting, financial, educational, construction, electrical, legal, and medical.)
    - The services are provided by individuals with those skills.
    - The services would typically need to be purchased by the organization if they had not been contributed.

Just because an individual has a specialized skill does not mean that the skill meets the criteria to be reported. For example, a CPA may volunteer for an organization in a position that does not require his or her CPA skills, create, or enhance a nonfinancial asset. Therefore, this contributed service would not be reported in the financial statements. However, for example, if the CPA contributes his or her services to

---

a position that requires those skills, and typically the organization would have to pay for those services, it would be reported in the financial statements.

Recognized contributed services should be reported as contribution revenue and as assets or expenses. Contributed services and promises to give services that do not meet the criteria should not be recognized. Recognized contributions should be measured at fair value. Contributions of services that create or enhance nonfinancial assets may be measured by referring to either the fair value of the services received or the fair value of the asset or of the asset enhancement resulting from the services. Fair value should be used for the measure regardless of whether the not-for-profit could afford to purchase the services at their fair value.

## KNOWLEDGE CHECK

1. Which is true of contributed services?

   a. Fair value should be used for the measure regardless of whether the not-for-profit could afford to purchase the services at their fair value.
   b. Contributed services that do not meet the criteria should still be recognized.
   c. Promises to give services that do not meet the criteria should still be recognized.
   d. Contributed services are not reported by not-for-profit organizations.

2. Which is true of contributed services?

   a. If a CPA contributes his or her services to a position that requires those skills, and typically the organization would have to pay for those services, it would be reported in the financial statements.
   b. If a CPA volunteers for an organization in a position that does not require his or her CPA skills or create or enhance a nonfinancial asset, it would be reported in the financial statements.
   c. Just because an individual has a specialized skill, means that the skill meets the criteria to be reported.
   d. All contributed services by a CPA should be reported.

Contributed services (and the related assets and expenses) should be recognized if employees of separately governed affiliated entities regularly perform services (in other than an advisory capacity) for and under the direction of the donee and the recognition criteria for contributed services are met.

## KNOWLEDGE CHECK

3. Which is true of contributed services?

   a. There are no disclosure requirements related to contributions of services.
   b. The FASB *Accounting Standards Codification* (ASC) 958, *Not-for-Profit Entities*, does not provide examples of applying the accounting concepts related to contributed services.
   c. Contributed services should be recognized if employees of separately governed affiliated entities regularly perform services (in other than an advisory capacity) for and under the direction of the donee and the recognition criteria for contributed services are met.
   d. Not-for-profits should not disclose contributed services that do not meet the recognition criteria.

### Examples in the FASB ASC

FASB ASC 958-605 provides examples of applying the accounting concepts related to contributed services. Selected aspects of four examples are illustrated in the following:

### Contributed Board of Trustee Services

A member of the board of trustees of a not-for-profit is a lawyer and occasionally in the capacity of a trustee provides advice on general business matters, including questions about business opportunities and risks and ethical, moral, and legal matters. The advice provided on legal matters is provided as a trustee in the role of a trustee, not as a lawyer, and the opinions generally are limited to routine matters. The lawyer generally suggests that the not-for-profit seek the opinion of its attorneys on substantive or complex legal questions. All of the not-for-profit's trustees serve without compensation, and most trustees have specialized expertise that makes their advice valuable to the not-for-profit. The trustee-lawyer also serves without compensation as a trustee for two other not-for-profits.

The trustee-lawyer's services are not recognized because the substantive or complex legal questions that require the specialized skills of a lawyer are referred to the not-for-profit's attorneys or because the advice provided by trustees typically would not be purchased if not provided by donation.

## Contributed Teaching Services

A university includes faculty, which are both compensated faculty members (approximately 80 percent) and uncompensated faculty members (approximately 20 percent) who are associated with religious orders and contribute their services. The performance of both compensated and uncompensated faculty members is regularly and similarly evaluated; both must meet the university's standards and both provide services in the same way.

The university would recognize both revenue and expense for the services contributed by the uncompensated faculty members. Teaching requires specialized skills; the religious personnel are qualified and trained to provide those skills; and the university typically would hire paid instructors if the religious personnel did not donate their services. The university could refer to the salaries it pays similarly-qualified compensated faculty members to determine fair value of the services received.

If the uncompensated faculty members were given a nominal stipend to help pay certain of their out-of-pocket expenses, the university still would recognize both revenue and expense for the services contributed. The contribution received would be measured at the fair value of the services received less the amount of the nominal stipend paid.

## Contributed Services to Construct a Building

A not-for-profit decides to construct a building on its property. It purchases architectural services, materials, permits, and so forth at a total cost of $400,000. A local construction entity contributes the necessary labor and equipment. An independent appraisal of the building (exclusive of land), obtained for insurance purposes, estimates its fair value at $725,000.

The not-for-profit would recognize contributed services. The fair value of the contributed services received could be determined by subtracting the cost of the purchased services, materials, and permits ($400,000) from the fair value of the asset created ($725,000), which results in contributed services received of $325,000. Alternatively, the amount the construction entity would have charged could be used if more readily available.

## Contributed Volunteer Services

A not-for-profit hospital provides short-term inpatient and outpatient care and also provides long-term care for the elderly. As part of the long-term care program, the hospital has organized a program whereby local high school students may contribute a minimum of 10 hours a week, from 3:00 p.m. to 6:00 p.m., to the hospital. These students are assigned various duties, such as visiting and talking with the patients, distributing books and magazines, reading, playing chess, and similar activities. The hospital does not pay for these services or similar services. The services are accepted as a way of enhancing or supplementing the quality of care and comfort provided to the elderly long-term care patients.

The hospital would not recognize the contributed services because the services the students provide do not require specialized skills nor would they typically need to be purchased if not provided by donation.

## Disclosures

The notes to the financial statements should include the following disclosures concerning contributions of services received during the period:

- The nature and extent of contributed services received by the not-for-profit.
- A description of the programs or activities for which the services were used.
- The amount of contributed services recognized during the period.

Not-for-profits are encouraged to report in the notes to the financial statements, if practical, the fair value of contributed services received but not recognized.

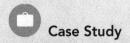

## Case Study

The United Fund of the New River Valley (UFNRV) is a local not-for-profit entity governed by people who volunteer to serve on the Board of Directors and other committees and teams. The UFNRV is focused on generating and providing the community with resources to build support for local human needs.

The UFNRV serves an area made up of four counties and three towns. The total population of this area is approximately 75,000 and contains a state university. The UFNRV raises approximately $1,000,000 a year and has an operating budget of $200,000. The remaining $800,000 is given out as grants to other not-for-profits in the area.

The UFNRV is governed by a 20 member Board of Directors. Members of the board receive no compensation for their services. The board is primarily made up of area business leaders and educators. There are four officers on the Board, including a volunteer treasurer who is appointed to a three-year term. The current treasurer is an accounting faculty member at the state university. She is a CPA and has a PhD in accounting. Her duties as treasurer are to sign all checks, review the monthly bank reconciliations and monthly financial reports. She also signs the audit representation letter. This year she has volunteered to help the organization document its internal control procedures. She has spent about 40 hours on this project.

Each year the UFNRV has a campaign kickoff event. The president of the organization has persuaded the coach of the state university's football team to be the speaker at the event. The coach has been very successful and usually receives a minimum of $5,000 for any speaking engagement. He has agreed to donate his time for this event.

The UFNRV is located in a small house owned by a local bank. The organization is responsible for all utilities, but pays no rent. This arrangement has been in effect for the last five years and should continue. However, there is no formal written agreement. On the Board of Directors is the owner of a small roofing company. The owner has worked out a deal with the bank that owns the building to replace the roof. The bank will buy the material and members of the Board will volunteer to provide the labor to install the roof. The owner of the roofing company will supervise the project.

**Case Study (continued)**

Case Study Exercise

Review the items listed in the following chart. Indicate which contributed services you believe should be recognized. If you believe that the service should be recognized also indicate how you might value the service.

| Item | Should the contributed service be recognized? If the service should be recognized, how might you value the service? |
| --- | --- |
| The normal duties of the treasurer | |
| The treasurer's work on documenting internal controls | |
| The football coach's speech | |
| The labor to install the new roof on the building | |

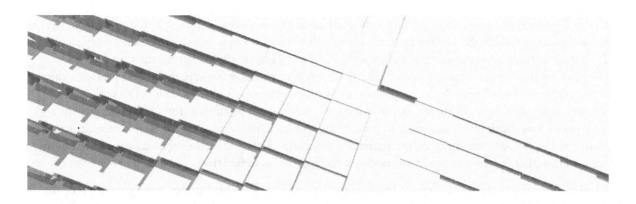

## Chapter 8

# SPLIT-INTEREST AGREEMENTS

## LEARNING OBJECTIVES

After completing this chapter, you should be able to do the following:

- Analyze the decisive characteristics of revocable and irrevocable split-interest agreements.
- Compare how different types of split-interest agreements are accounted for.
- Differentiate the five types of split-interest agreements.

## TECHNICAL BACKGROUND INFORMATION

Not-for-profit entities sometimes enter into trust or other arrangements with donors where the not-for-profit entity will share the benefits of such trust or other arrangement with other beneficiaries. Such trust or other arrangements are referred to as *split-interest agreements*. As shown in the following illustration, there are five types of split-interest agreements commonly used by not-for-profit entities.

| Charitable Remainder Trusts | | Charitable Gift Annuities |
|---|---|---|
| Charitable Lead Trusts | Types of Split-Interest Agreements | Pooled (Life) Income Funds |
| Perpetual Trusts Held by Third Parties | | |

Under a split-interest agreement, a donor makes an initial gift to a trust, a fiscal agent, or directly to the not-for-profit, in which the not-for-profit has a beneficial interest but is not the sole beneficiary. The terms of some agreements do not allow donors to revoke their gifts; other agreements may be revocable by donors in certain situations. The time period covered by the agreement is expressed either as a specific number of years (or in perpetuity) or as the remaining life of an individual or individuals designated by the donor. The assets are invested and administered by the not-for-profit, a trustee, or a fiscal agent, and distributions are made to a beneficiary or beneficiaries during the term of the agreement. At the end of the agreement's term, the remaining assets covered by the agreement are distributed to or retained by either the not-for-profit or another beneficiary or beneficiaries.

Under a *lead-interest* agreement, the not-for-profit entity receives the distributions during the term of the agreement. Under a *remainder-interest* agreement, the donor (or others designated by the donor) receives the distributions during the term of the agreement; however, the not-for-profit entity receives all or a portion of the assets remaining at the end of the agreement's term. Under either agreement, the donor may impose restrictions on the use of all or a portion of the assets.

In accordance with FASB *Accounting Standards Codification* (ASC) 958, *Not-for-Profit Entities*, the contribution portion of a split-interest agreement (that is, the part that represents the unconditional transfer of assets in a voluntary nonreciprocal transaction) should be recognized as revenue or gain. [As discussed in the FASB ASC glossary definition of *contribution*, the term *contribution revenue* in the FASB ASC is used to apply to transactions that are part of the entity's ongoing major or central activities (revenues), or are peripheral or incidental to the entity (gains).] In accordance with FASB ASC 958, a contribution should be measured at its fair value.

Recognition of split-interest agreements also requires assets and liabilities to be measured initially at fair value, and, in certain cases, requires them to be remeasured at fair value subsequently. FASB ASC 820, *Fair Value Measurement*, establishes a framework for measuring fair value. Present value techniques can be used possibly to measure the contribution revenue and obligation to other beneficiaries of a split-interest agreement. Other valuation techniques are also available, as described in FASB ASC 820.

## Revocable Agreements

FASB ASC 958 discusses recognition and measurement of revocable split-interest agreements. The following illustration shows certain key concepts related to revocable split-interest agreements.

### Key Concepts Related to Revocable Split-Interest Agreements

 Revocable split-interest agreements should be accounted for as intentions to give.

 Assets received by a not-for-profit acting as a trustee under a revocable split-interest agreement should be recognized at fair value when received as assets and as refundable advances. If those assets are investments, they should be recognized in conformity with FASB ASC 958-320 or 958-325 as appropriate.

 Contribution revenue for the assets received should be recognized when the agreements become irrevocable or when the assets are distributed to the not-for-profit for its unconditional use, whichever occurs first.

 Income earned on assets held under revocable agreements that is not available for the not-for-profit's unconditional use, and any subsequent adjustments to the carrying value of those assets, should be recognized as adjustments to the assets and as refundable advances.

## Distinctions in Split-Interest Agreements

Earlier, we noted that there are five types of split-interest agreements commonly used by not-for-profit entities. The following illustration offers more details about the five types:

| | |
|---|---|
| Charitable Lead Trusts | A charitable lead trust is an agreement in which the donor establishes a trust that will make specific distributions to the not-for-profit entity over a specified period. The distributions may be for a specific amount or for a fixed percentage of the trust's fair market value. At the end of the agreement, the trust's assets are paid to the donor or to other beneficiaries designated by the donor. |
| Perpetual Trusts Held by Third Parties | A perpetual trust held by a third party is an agreement where the donor establishes a perpetual trust that will be administered by an individual or organization other than the not-for-profit entity. The not-for-profit entity has an irrevocable right to receive the income earned on the trust assets in perpetuity. However, the not-for-profit entity will never receive the assets (or principal) held in trust. |
| Charitable Remainder Trusts | A charitable remainder trust is an arrangement in which a donor establishes a trust with specified distributions to be made to a designated beneficiary or beneficiaries over the trust's term. Upon termination of the trust, a not-for-profit entity receives the assets remaining in the trust. |
| Charitable Gift Annuities | A charitable gift annuity is an arrangement between a donor and a not-for-profit entity in which the donor contributes assets to the organization in exchange for a promise by the organization to pay a fixed amount for a specified period of time to the donor or to individuals or organizations designated by the donor. The agreements are similar to charitable remainder annuity trusts except that no trust exists, the assets received are held as general assets of the not-for-profit entity, and the annuity liability is a general obligation of the organization. |
| Pooled (Life) Income Funds | Some not-for-profit entities form, invest, and manage pooled (or life) income funds. These funds are divided into units and contributions of many donors' life income gifts are pooled and invested as a group. Donors are assigned a specific number of units based on the proportion of the fair value of their contributions to the total fair value of the pooled income fund on the date of the donor's entry to the pooled fund. Until a donor's death, the donor (or the donor's designated beneficiary or beneficiaries) is paid, the actual income (as defined under the arrangement) earned on the donor's assigned units. Upon the donor's death, the value of these assigned units reverts to the not-for-profit entity. |

## KNOWLEDGE CHECK

1.  Which is true of perpetual trusts held by third parties?

    a.  The not-for-profit entity has an irrevocable right to receive the income earned on the trust assets in perpetuity.
    b.  The not-for-profit entity will always receive the assets held in trust.
    c.  A perpetual trust held by a third party is an agreement where the donor establishes a perpetual trust that will be administered by the not-for-profit entity.
    d.  A perpetual trust is similar to a charitable gift annuity.

2.  Which is true of charitable remainder trusts?

    a.  A charitable remainder trust is an arrangement in which a donor establishes a trust with specified distributions to be made to a designated beneficiary or beneficiaries over the trust's term.
    b.  Upon termination of the trust, a not-for-profit entity does not receive the assets remaining in the trust.
    c.  Charitable remainder trusts are never used by not-for-profit entities.
    d.  Under a charitable remainder trust, the not-for-profit receives distributions during the life of the trust.

3.  Which is true of charitable gift annuities?

    a.  The agreements are similar to charitable remainder annuity trusts except that a trust exists.
    b.  The assets received are not held as general assets of the not-for-profit entity.
    c.  The annuity liability is a general obligation of the organization.
    d.  Charitable gift annuities are similar to charitable remainder annuity trusts, and there is a trust document.

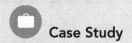 **Case Study**

Review both of the following situations and answer the questions presented.

**Situation 1**

University A has an alumnus who wants to give the institution $400,000 to be invested by the university and pay him $12,000 per year for the remainder of his life. Upon his death, his will may give the residual of the funds to the University. His life expectancy as of the date of the gift is approximately 10 years. Assume that the present value of $12,000 paid out at the end of each year for a 10-year period is $92,700.

    1.   What type of split-interest arrangement is described in Situation 1?

    2.   What journal entry would University A record at the creation of the arrangement?

**Situation 2**

University A has a board member who wants to give $400,000 to the University and have the university receive $12,000 per year for the remainder of his life. Upon his death, the residual of the funds will go to the YWCA of Anywhere County. His life expectancy as of the date of the gift is approximately 10 years. Assume that the present value of $12,000 paid out at the end of each year for a 10-year period is $92,700.

    1.   What type of split-interest arrangement is described in Situation 2?

    2.   What would be the journal entry for the creation of this trust?

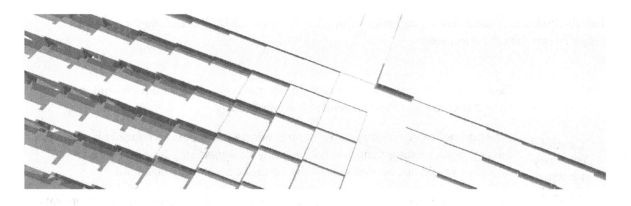

## Chapter 9

# ASSESSING INTERNAL CONTROL DEFICIENCIES

## LEARNING OBJECTIVES

After completing this chapter, you should be able to do the following:

- Identify internal control, internal control elements, and internal control risk as related to fraud.
- Identify key issues in evaluating and reporting internal control deficiencies as relates to fraud.
- Identify the auditor's evaluation of internal control deficiencies as relates to fraud.
- Identify the auditor's responsibility as it relates to fraud.

## TECHNICAL BACKGROUND INFORMATION

For purposes of this chapter, we will discuss the generally accepted auditing standards (GAAS) audit of an organization's financial statements, which, of significance to this course chapter would include an examination of the design and operating effectiveness of an entity's internal control(s). Specifically, this chapter addresses internal control, the elements of internal control and internal control deficiencies as relates to fraud in not-for-profit entities.

This discussion uses the following definitions from AU-C section 265, *Communicating Internal Control Related Matters Identified in an Audit*:

| | |
|---|---|
| Control Deficiency in Internal Control | Exists when the design or operation of internal controls does not prevent, or detect and correct, misstatements on a timely basis.<br><br>A design deficiency exists when a control needed to meet the control objective is missing or an existing control is not properly designed so that the control objective would not be met even if the control operated as designed.<br><br>An operation deficiency exists when a properly designed control does not operate as designed effectively. This can include when the person performing the control does not have the necessary authority or competence to perform the control. |
| Material Weakness | A deficiency or combination of deficiencies, in internal control, such that there is a reasonable possibility that a material misstatement of the entity's financial statements will not be prevented, or detected and corrected, on a timely basis. |
| Significant Deficiency | A deficiency, or a combination of deficiencies, in internal control that is less severe than a material weakness, yet important enough to merit attention by those charged with governance. |

## Internal Control and its Elements

Internal control is a system of policies and procedures designed to provide reliable financial reporting free of material misstatement, effective and efficient operations, and compliance with applicable laws and regulations.

It is important that the auditor understand the organization's internal controls in order to assess control risk, or, by definition, the failure of internal control(s) to detect a material misstatement. The auditor's assessment of internal control risk is essential for the auditor to design the nature and extent of audit procedures properly to address audit risk. Together, the auditor's understanding of the organization, its environment, and its internal control is the foundation on which the auditor builds the audit.

Internal control consists of five key interrelated elements as follows:

## Elements of Internal Control

| CE | RA | IC | CA | M |
|---|---|---|---|---|
| Control Environment | Risk Assessment & Management | Information & Communication Systems | Control Activities | Monitoring |

## Control Environment

The control environment is the attitude toward internal control and control consciousness established and maintained by the management and the employees of the entity. Management is responsible for the internal control of an organization. Internal control is the product of management's philosophy, style, and supportive attitude, as well as the competence, ethical values, integrity, and morale of organization personnel. Organization structure and accountability relationships are key factors in the control environment.

## Risk Assessment and Management

Risk ultimately affects or potentially impairs the not-for-profit entity's ability to succeed in its accounting and reporting objectives. Ultimately, audit risk is the risk that an auditor may issue an unqualified report due to the auditor's failure to detect a material omission, error, or intentional miscalculation (specifically, fraud). Risk assessment is the process of identifying and evaluating such risk. For example, the auditor may consider obstacles, worst-case scenarios, legislative change, employee turnover, and more in assessing and evaluating risk. Managing risk is an activity of the not-for-profit entity's management whereby management should consider how best to disposition identified risks. This can include the decision to accept the risk, reduce the risk to acceptable levels or avoid the risk altogether. To have reasonable assurance that the organization will achieve its objectives, management should ensure each risk is assessed and handled properly.

## Information and Communication Systems

Information should be communicated to management and other employees in an effective (form and content needed) and efficient (on a timely basis) manner. Communication is the exchange of this information between and among people and organizations to support decisions and coordinate activities that assist the entity or personnel in performing responsibilities. Communication occurs with both internal and external parties, such as employees and grantors, of a not-for-profit entity.

## Control Activities

Control activities are comprised of policies, procedures, and processes placed into effect by the not-for-profit entity to mitigate or reduce the accounting and reporting risks that can impede the accomplishment of the organization's objectives and mission. These manual and electronic tools include, by way of example, the not-for-profit's documentation, approval and validation practices, the separation of duties, financial reporting, and computer system preventive measures. Management should establish control activities to accomplish the organization's objectives and mission effectively and efficiently.

## Monitoring

Monitoring is the review of an organization's activities and transactions to assess the quality of performance over time and to determine the effectiveness of the controls. Management should focus monitoring efforts on internal controls and the achievement of the not-for-profit entity's objectives. Control activities, the control environment, communication, and an ongoing assessment of risk, including the consideration of risk for potential fraud, are areas to consider. All employees should be involved in monitoring and have an understanding of risk tolerance levels in performing their activities to maximize effectiveness.

## Additional Discussion

Internal control is affected by management, personnel, and those charged with governance (usually a board of directors or trustees of a not-for-profit entity). The system of internal control is also influenced by the organization's size and culture, as well as management's philosophy and style, and the users of the financial statements.

---

Internal control encompasses several financial accounting and reporting objectives, such as [by way of example] safeguarding assets against unauthorized acquisition, use, or disposition. Auditors should assess the risk that internal control(s) will not prevent or detect and correct on a timely basis a material misstatement due to fraud.

Management is responsible for internal controls. The board of directors, in addition to management, of a not-for-profit entity can be an integral part of the organization's internal control system. External parties to the organization, however, are not considered part of the organization's internal control unless those external parties have been hired specifically to be part of the internal control of the entity. Users of the financial statements, regulatory agencies, and the auditor cannot be part of the organization's internal control, although external parties can exert influence on an organization's internal control, as previously stated.

---

## KNOWLEDGE CHECK

1. Which is true of a system of internal control?

    a. It is a system is affected by management and outside vendors.

    b. It is a system is affected by current and former personnel.

    c. It is a system is affected by economic and industry factors.

    d. It is a system is affected by those charged with governance.

### Evaluation of Internal Control

The auditor does not have to go looking for deficiencies in internal control. That is, auditors are not required to design audit procedures specifically to detect deficiencies in internal control. To do so would be beyond the scope of an audit in accordance with GAAS and would most likely not be an efficient audit. However, the auditor may come across deficiencies in the performance of audit procedures. When the auditor comes across deficiencies, he or she is required to evaluate the deficiencies to assess their severity and follow requirements regarding reporting the deficiencies to management and to those charged with governance.

In gaining an understanding of the organization's internal control, the auditor may identify deficiencies in the design. Deficiencies in the design are elements of the system of internal control, where there is nothing to prevent or detect a misstatement or noncompliance.

---

## KNOWLEDGE CHECK

2. Which is true of evaluating internal control?

    a. The auditor has to go looking for deficiencies in internal control.

    b. Auditors are required to design audit procedures specifically to detect deficiencies in internal control.

    c. Auditors are required to report all control deficiencies identified.

    d. The auditor may come across deficiencies in the performance of audit procedures.

Because internal control is a system of policies and procedures designed to provide reliable financial reporting, effective and efficient operations, and compliance with applicable laws and regulations, evaluating those factors is a good place to begin evaluation of internal control. The following for example:

- *Consider if the system of internal control provides reliable financial reporting* – If the financial statements, including disclosures, require no adjustment by the auditor or assistance from the auditor, there is an indication that there may not be reportable deficiencies in internal control. To the extent the financial statements include proposed adjustments by the auditor, the auditor needs to evaluate if there are reportable deficiencies.
- *Consider if the system of internal control is promoting effective and efficient operations* –If the auditor finds instances where control activities or monitoring, for example, have not been effective in preventing or detecting the errors or fraud they were designed to prevent or detect, the auditor needs to evaluate if there are reportable deficiencies.
- *Consider if the system of internal control has ensured compliance with applicable laws and regulations* – For not-for-profit entities, this may also include compliance with grant provisions or donor stipulations. If the auditor determines there was noncompliance in any of those areas, the auditor needs to evaluate if there are reportable deficiencies.

## KNOWLEDGE CHECK

3. Which is true of evaluating internal control?

    a. When the auditor comes across deficiencies, he or she is required to evaluate the deficiencies to assess their severity and follow requirements regarding reporting the deficiencies.
    b. In gaining an understanding of the organization's internal control, the auditor typically does not identify deficiencies in the design or operation of internal control.
    c. In gaining an understanding of the organization's internal control, the auditor is required to test internal controls to support control risk.
    d. Deficiencies in the design of internal control are elements of the system of internal control not operating as intended.

## Evaluation of Deficiencies in Internal Control

A deficiency in internal control exists when there is a reasonable possibility that the entity's controls will fail to prevent, or detect and correct, a misstatement of an account balance or financial statement disclosure. When the auditor has determined such a deficiency exists, the auditor must then evaluate the severity of the deficiency. Key considerations include the likelihood and the magnitude of a potential misstatement.

The auditor's assessment of the severity of a deficiency does not depend on, or require, that a misstatement actually occurred. Rather, the severity, or level of risk, is the auditor's assessment of the likelihood.

The magnitude of a misstatement refers to its potential quantitative or qualitative materiality. When a misstatement has been identified by the auditor, then the auditor should consider that there is no longer a possibility that the organization's controls will fail to prevent or detect a misstatement. Instead, there is a reality that the organization's controls did fail to prevent or detect a misstatement. The auditor has identified not just the potential for a misstatement, but has also identified an actual misstatement. The auditor then needs to consider the magnitude of the misstatement.

For example, if the auditor proposes three adjustments and an additional disclosure to the financial statements, the auditor has identified that the likelihood is more than a reasonable possibility since the misstatements did in fact occur. The auditor has also identified there is more than a potential for misstatement as the misstatement did happen. The auditor then needs to consider the magnitude of the misstatements (including the omitted disclosure).

The auditor needs to consider beyond identified misstatements. The auditor needs to consider potential misstatements that could happen based on the design or operation of internal control.

Factors that affect the magnitude of a misstatement that might result from a deficiency or deficiencies include, but are not limited to, the following:

- The financial statement amounts or total of transactions exposed to the deficiency.
- The volume of activity (in the current period or expected in future periods) in the account or class of transactions exposed to the deficiency.

## KNOWLEDGE CHECK

4.  Which is true of evaluating deficiencies in internal control?

    a.  The severity of a deficiency depends entirely on whether a misstatement actually occurred.
    b.  To the extent the financial statements include proposed adjustments by the auditor, the auditor needs to evaluate if there are reportable deficiencies.
    c.  The magnitude of a misstatement refers to its potential quantitative materiality.
    d.  The auditor should only consider misstatements actually found during the audit.

5.  Which statement is the best summary of evaluating deficiencies in internal control?

    a.  The auditor needs to consider misstatements that the client corrected during the audit period.
    b.  The auditor needs to consider misstatements that could be prevented because of the design of internal control.
    c.  The auditor is not required to consider misstatements that could happen as a result of failed internal controls.
    d.  The auditor needs to consider misstatements that could happen based on the operation of internal control.

Risk factors affect whether there is a reasonable possibility that a deficiency, or a combination of deficiencies, will result in a misstatement of an account balance or disclosure. The factors include, but are not limited to, the following:

| The nature of the financial statement accounts, classes of transactions, disclosures, and assertions involved | | The susceptibility of the related asset or liability to loss or fraud |
| --- | --- | --- |
| The interaction among the deficiencies | **Risk Factors** | The possible future consequences of the deficiency |
| The subjectivity, complexity, or extent of judgment required to determine the amount involved | | The interaction or relationship of the control with other controls |

## KNOWLEDGE CHECK

6. Which is true of risk factors?

    a. Risk factors include the susceptibility of the related asset or liability to loss or fraud.
    b. Risk factors include the nature of internal controls implemented.
    c. Risk factors include the possible future changes in the control.
    d. Risk factors include the interaction or relationship of the control with generally accepted accounting principles.

The evaluation of whether a deficiency presents a reasonable possibility of misstatement may be made without quantifying the probability of occurrence as a specific percentage or range.

Multiple deficiencies that affect the same significant account or disclosure, relevant assertion, or component of internal control increase the likelihood of material misstatement and may, in combination, constitute a significant deficiency or a material weakness, even though such deficiencies individually may be less severe. Therefore, the auditor should determine whether deficiencies that affect the same significant account or disclosure, relevant assertion, or component of internal control collectively result in a significant deficiency or a material weakness.

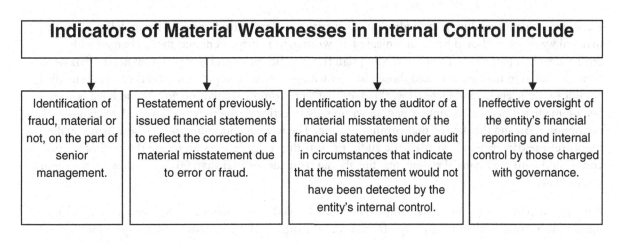

## Indicators of Material Weaknesses in Internal Control include

| Identification of fraud, material or not, on the part of senior management. | Restatement of previously-issued financial statements to reflect the correction of a material misstatement due to error or fraud. | Identification by the auditor of a material misstatement of the financial statements under audit in circumstances that indicate that the misstatement would not have been detected by the entity's internal control. | Ineffective oversight of the entity's financial reporting and internal control by those charged with governance. |
| --- | --- | --- | --- |

If the auditor determines that a deficiency, or a combination of deficiencies, is not a material weakness, the auditor should consider whether prudent officials, having knowledge of the same facts and circumstances, would likely reach the same conclusion.

## KNOWLEDGE CHECK

7. Which is true of evaluating deficiencies in internal control?

   a. The auditor should determine whether deficiencies that affect the same significant account or disclosure, relevant assertion, or component of internal control collectively result in a significant deficiency or a material weakness.
   b. The evaluation of whether a deficiency presents a reasonable possibility of misstatement cannot be made without quantifying the probability of occurrence as a specific percentage or range.
   c. In rare cases, the probability of a small misstatement will be greater than the probability of a large misstatement.
   d. Deficiencies that affect the same significant account or disclosure should only be evaluated individually.

### Compensating Controls

When performing substantive procedures or tests of the operating effectiveness of controls, the auditor may obtain evidence that a control does not operate effectively, for example, by identifying a misstatement that was not prevented, or detected and corrected by the control. Management may inform the auditor, or the auditor may otherwise become aware, of the existence of compensating controls that, if effective, may limit the severity of the deficiency and prevent it from being a significant deficiency or a material weakness. In these circumstances, although the auditor is not required to consider the effects of compensating controls for purposes of communicating internal control related matters identified in an audit, the auditor may consider the effects of compensating controls related to a deficiency in operation provided the auditor has tested the compensating controls for operating effectiveness as part of the financial statement audit. It is important to distinguish that compensating controls can limit the severity of the deficiency, although they do not eliminate the deficiency (or deficiencies).

### Communication of Deficiencies in Internal Control

Deficiencies identified during the audit that upon evaluation are considered significant deficiencies or material weaknesses should be communicated, in writing, to management and those charged with governance as a part of each audit, including significant deficiencies and material weaknesses that were communicated to management and those charged with governance in previous audits not yet remedied. Significant deficiencies and material weaknesses that were communicated previously and have not yet been remediated may be communicated, in writing, by referring to the previously-issued written communication and the date of that communication. The written communication is best made by the report release date, which is the date the auditor grants the entity permission to use the auditor's report in connection with the financial statements, but should be made no later than 60 days following the report release date.

For some matters, early communication to management and those charged with governance may be important because of their relative significance and the urgency for corrective follow-up action.

Accordingly, the auditor may decide to communicate certain matters during the audit. These matters need not be communicated in writing during the audit, but significant deficiencies and material weaknesses ultimately should be included in a written communication (as discussed in the preceding paragraph), even if such significant deficiencies or material weaknesses were remediated during the audit.

The existence of significant deficiencies or material weaknesses may already be known to management and may represent a conscious decision by management or those charged with governance to accept the risk associated with the deficiencies because of cost or other considerations. Management is responsible for making decisions concerning costs to be incurred and related benefits. The auditor's responsibility to communicate significant deficiencies and material weaknesses exists regardless of management's decisions.

Nothing precludes the auditor from communicating to management and those charged with governance over other matters related to an entity's internal control. For example, the auditor may communicate the following:

- Matters the auditor believes to be of potential benefit to the entity, such as recommendations for operational or administrative efficiency, or for improving controls.
- Deficiencies that are not significant deficiencies or material weaknesses.

If other matters are communicated orally, the auditor should document the communication.

## KNOWLEDGE CHECK

8. Which is true of the auditor's evaluation of control deficiencies?

    a. The auditor's evaluation involves considering whether compensating controls exist.
    b. The auditor's evaluation is only effective when management brings deficiencies to the auditor's attention.
    c. The auditor's evaluation is dependent upon whether the control has been tested.
    d. The auditor's evaluation process includes communication with governance.

### Summary of the Auditor's Evaluation

The following is a highly-summarized view of the auditor's evaluation once a potential deficiency in internal control has been identified:

## Summary of the Auditor's Evaluation

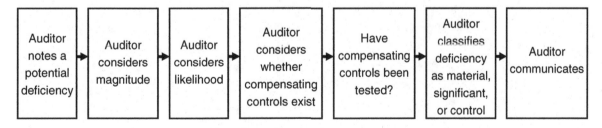

# KNOWLEDGE CHECK

9. Which is true of the auditor's evaluation of control deficiencies?

    a. The auditor's evaluation involves noting a potential deficiency.
    b. The auditor's evaluation involves the auditor considering magnitude.
    c. The auditor's evaluation involves the auditor considering likelihood.
    d. All of the above.

## Lesson from Peer Review Results

Results from peer review over the past few years have consistently identified failure to communicate, or communicate properly, internal control deficiencies as one of the most common matters in an audit. Auditors should be aware that communicating internal control deficiencies in a management letter, or in an "opportunity to improve" letter, may not meet professional standards.

---

### Case Study

#### Case Study Exercise

Isolated But Dedicated is a small not-for-profit audit client that has only one person in charge of the accounting and reporting functions. Through your understanding of controls over cash disbursements, you observe a lack of segregation of duties, which is a deficiency in internal control. In assessing the severity of the deficiency in internal control, you consider whether complementary, redundant, or compensating controls exist. Through obtaining your understanding of internal control, you have learned that a board member signs all checks, reviewing invoices that support the disbursement before signing. The signed checks are returned to the client to be mailed. The bank sends the bank statement directly to the board member, who reviews the bank statement and returned checks. The bank statement is then given to the client for reconciliation.

How might your assessment of the severity of this deficiency in internal control be affected by the effectiveness of the compensating controls performed by the board members?

---

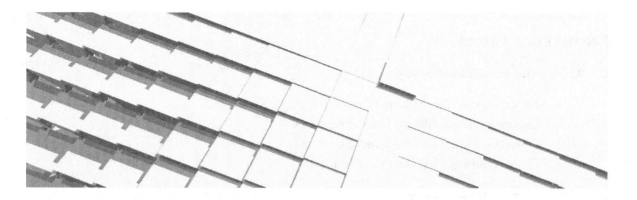

# Chapter 10

# CAPITAL CAMPAIGNS AND SPECIAL EVENTS

## LEARNING OBJECTIVES

After completing this chapter, you should be able to do the following:

- Identify key accounting issues related to measurement of contributions related to pledges and special event costs associated with a capital campaign.
- Identify the use of present value techniques in measuring unconditional promises to give cash that is expected to be collected in more than one year.

## TECHNICAL BACKGROUND INFORMATION

Many not-for-profit entities depend on contributions to pay for major capital projects and to build endowment funds. Such organizations often will have a capital campaign that will last several years and will result in donations that are received over a period of time. Donations can take the form of things such as cash or other assets—including securities, land, buildings, use of facilities or utilities, materials and supplies, intangible assets, services, and unconditional promises to give those items in the future.

# KNOWLEDGE CHECK

1. Which is true of capital campaigns?

    a. Donations can take the form of cash.
    b. Donations cannot take the form of securities.
    c. Donations cannot take the form of land.
    d. Capital campaigns last less than a year.

2. Which is true of capital campaigns?

    a. Donations cannot take the form of buildings.
    b. Donations can take the form of the use of facilities or utilities.
    c. Donations cannot take the form of materials and supplies.
    d. Capital campaigns must last a year.

3. Which is true of capital campaigns?

    a. Donations cannot take the form of intangible assets.
    b. Donations cannot take the form of services.
    c. Donations can take the form of unconditional promises to give items in the future.
    d. Capital campaigns must last for five years to be considered a capital campaign.

Provided that sufficient, verifiable evidence exists that a promise was made and received, an unconditional promise to give shall be recognized when the promise is received. A common issue with such contributions received as part of a capital campaign is how these contributions should be measured (as they typically will not be received for some time).

## Measurement of Contributions

**Fair Market Value and Valuation Techniques**. Contribution revenue should be measured at the fair value of the assets or services received or promised or the fair value of the liabilities satisfied. Contributions arising from unconditional promises to give that are expected to be collected within one year of the financial statement date may be measured at their net realizable value. FASB ASC 820, *Fair Value Measurement*, defines fair value and establishes a framework for measuring fair value.

# Discussion of FASB ASC 820

See Author Comment

## Definition of Fair Value

FASB ASC 820 defines fair value as "the price that would be received to sell an asset or paid to transfer a liability in an orderly transaction between market participants at the measurement date." That definition retains the exchange price notion in earlier definitions of fair value, but it clarifies that the exchange price is the price in a hypothetical transaction at the measurement date in the market in which the reporting entity would transact for the asset or liability. A fair value measurement assumes that the transaction to sell the asset or transfer the liability occurs in the principal market for the asset or liability or, in the absence of a principal market, the most advantageous market for the asset or liability. FASB ASC 820 provides that a fair value measurement of an asset assumes the highest and best use of the asset by market participants, considering the use of the asset that is physically possible, legally permissible, and financially feasible at the measurement date.

## Valuation Techniques

FASB ASC 820 describes the valuation techniques that should be used to measure fair value consistent with the market approach, income approach and/or cost approach, as follows:

- The market approach uses prices and other relevant information generated by market transactions involving identical or comparable assets or liabilities. Valuation techniques consistent with the market approach include matrix pricing and often use market multiples derived from a set of comparables.
- The income approach uses valuation techniques to convert future amounts (including cash flows or earnings) to a single present value amount (discounted). The measurement is based discount rates applied to future cash flows, where the cumulative discounted value, or present value, is indicated by current market expectations about those future cash flows or earnings. Valuation techniques consistent with the income approach include present value techniques, option-pricing models and the multi-period excess earnings method.
- The cost approach is based on the amount that currently would be required to replace the service capacity of an asset (often referred to as current replacement cost). Fair value is determined based on the cost to a market participant (buyer) to acquire or construct a substitute asset of comparable utility, adjusted for obsolescence.

## KNOWLEDGE CHECK

4. Which is true of the market approach?

   a. Valuation techniques consistent with the market approach include matrix pricing and often use market multiples derived from a set of comparables.
   b. The market approach does not use prices or other relevant information generated by market transactions involving identical or comparable assets or liabilities.
   c. Present value of future cash flows is an example of a market approach.
   d. The cost approach is an example of a market approach.

**Contributed Assets.** The fair value of contributed services that create or enhance nonfinancial assets should be estimated based on (*a*) the fair value of the services received or (*b*) the fair value of the assets created (or the change in the fair value of the asset that is being enhanced), whichever is more readily determinable.

Major uncertainties about the existence of value of a contributed asset may indicate that a contribution should not be recognized. Such uncertainties are often present when an item has no use other than for scientific or educational research or for its historical significance. Examples of such items include flora, fauna, photographs, and objects identified with historic persons, places, or events.

**Restricted Assets.** A fair value measurement should be determined based on the assumptions that market participants would use in pricing the asset, including, under certain circumstances, assumptions about the effect of a restriction on the sale or use of an asset, if market participants would consider the effect of the restriction in pricing the asset. FASB ASC 820-10-55-51, *Example 6: Restricted Assets*, explains that restrictions that are an attribute of an asset, and therefore would transfer to a market participant, are the only restrictions reflected in fair value. Donor restrictions that are specific to the donee are reflected in the classification of net assets, not in the measurement of fair value.

**Measurement of [Formerly] Conditional Contributions.** Promises to give that are deemed unconditional are not recognized in the financial statements of the not-for-profit. Where a promise to give has not previously been recognized as contribution revenue because it was conditional, fair value should be measured when the conditions are met.

The present value of the future cash flows is one valuation technique for measuring the fair value of contributions arising from unconditional promises to give cash; other valuation techniques also are available, as described in FASB ASC 820. The following example illustrates the use of present value techniques for initial recognition and measurement of unconditional promises to give cash that are expected to be collected one year or more after the financial statement date.

## Initial Recognition of Unconditional Promises to Give Cash Facts

- A not-for-profit entity receives a promise (or promises from a group of homogeneous donors) to give $100 in five years
- The anticipated future cash flows from the promise(s) are $70
- The present value of the future cash flows is $50

### Solution

debit Contributions Receivable $70
    credit Contribution Revenue – Temporarily Restricted $50
    credit Discount on Contributions Receivable $20

(To report contributions receivable and revenue using a present value technique to measure fair value.)

[Note: Some not-for-profits may use a subsidiary ledger to retain information concerning the $100 face amount of contributions promised in order to monitor collections of contributions promised.]

If present value techniques are used, the fair value of contributions arising from unconditional promises to give noncash assets might be determined based on the present value of the projected fair value of the underlying noncash assets at the date and in the quantities that those assets are expected to be received, if the date is one year or more after the financial statement date. [Both the (*a*) likelihood of the promise being fulfilled and (*b*) future fair value of those underlying assets, such as the future fair value per share of a promised equity security, should be considered in determining the future amount to be discounted.] In cases in which the future fair value of the underlying asset is difficult to determine, the fair value of an unconditional promise to give noncash assets may be based on the fair value of the underlying asset at the date of initial recognition. (No discount for the time value of money should be reported if an asset's fair value at the date of initial recognition is used to measure the fair value of the contribution.)

If present value techniques are used to measure the fair value of unconditional promises to give, a not-for-profit entity should determine the amount and timing of the future cash flows of unconditional promises to give cash (or, for promises to give noncash assets, the quantity and nature of assets expected to be received). In making that determination, not-for-profit entities should consider all the elements in paragraph 820-10 of the FASB ASC, including when the receivable is expected to be collected, the creditworthiness of the other parties, the organization's past collection experience, and its policies concerning the enforcement of promises to give, expectations about possible variations in the amount and/or timing of the cash flows (that is, the uncertainty inherent in the cash flows), and other factors concerning the receivable's collectibility.

## Special Fundraising Events Activities and Costs

**Fundraising and Special Event Activities.** Per the FASB ASC glossary, fundraising activities are activities undertaken to induce potential donors to contribute money, securities, services, materials, facilities, other assets, or time. Activities include publicizing and conducting fundraising campaigns; maintaining donor mailing lists; conducting special fundraising events; preparing and distributing fundraising materials, instructions, and other materials; and conducting other activities involved with soliciting contributions from individuals, foundations, government agencies, and others. Fundraising activities include soliciting contributions of services from individuals, regardless of whether those services meet the recognition criteria for contributions. The financial statements should disclose total fundraising expenses.

**Fundraising and Special Event Costs.** Per FASB ASC 958, *Not-for-Profit Entities*, fundraising costs, including the cost of special fundraising events, are incurred to persuade potential donors to make contributions to a not-for-profit and should be expensed as incurred. Costs are incurred when the item or service has been received. Fundraising costs incurred in one period, such as those made to obtain bequests, compile a mailing list of prospective contributors, or solicit contributions in a direct-response activity, may result in contributions that will be received in future periods. These costs also should be expensed as incurred.

Some expenses are directly related to, and can be assigned to, a single major program or service or a single supporting activity. Other expenses relate to more than one program or supporting activity or to a combination of programs and supporting services. These expenses should be allocated among the appropriate functions. Examples include a direct mail solicitation that combines fundraising with program activities (subject to certain provisions in the accounting literature), salaries of persons who perform more than one kind of service and the rental of a building used for various programs and supporting activities.

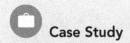
**Case Study**

Case Study Background Information

Dublin College is a private not-for-profit institution located in the mountains of Virginia. The college enrolls approximately 1,000 students. In addition to tuition, the college depends on contributions to help fund general operations and several specific activities. Annual tuition and fees for the college are $32,000 a year.

The college has just started a fundraising capital campaign to build a new science building. The college hopes to raise $2,500,000 in contributions restricted for the building. The capital campaign is anticipated to last three years.

The college kicked off their capital campaign with a special fundraising event as part of homecoming weekend. Catering, promotional materials, and entertainment for the event cost $25,000. In addition, the college purchased and received several exterior banners promoting the capital campaign that will be used over the next three years at a cost of $15,000.

During the event the following unconditional promises to give were received:

- 200 people pledged $100 each to be paid within one year. Based on past experience, the college expects to collect 95% of this amount.
- Twenty people joined the President's Club by pledging $10,000 each to be paid at the end of three years. The college expects to collect 90% ($180,000) of this amount. The college estimates the present value of the $180,000 to be $155,000.

Dublin College has adopted a policy to measure unconditional promises to give expected to be collected within one year at their net realizable value. Other unconditional promises to give are measured using a present value technique.

**Case Study (continued)**

Review the questions listed in the following chart related to Dublin College. Use the right column to answer each question.

| Question | Answer |
|---|---|
| What portion of the $40,000 costs related to the special fundraising event should be expensed? | |
| How would you prepare the journal entry for the 200 people who pledged $100 each to be paid within one year? | |
| How would you prepare the journal entry for the twenty people who pledged $10,000 each to be paid in three years? | |

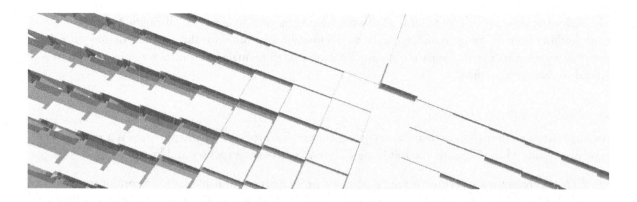

## Chapter 11

# FUNDRAISING EVENTS AND MEMBERSHIP

## LEARNING OBJECTIVES

After completing this chapter, you should be able to do the following:

- Determine how certain resource inflows stemming from a fundraising event should be reported as contributions or exchange transactions.
- Identify how membership dues should be reported.

## TECHNICAL BACKGROUND INFORMATION

Almost all not-for-profits conduct some type of fundraising event. We have all been invited to some type of bake sale, spaghetti supper, concert, annual gala, and more and more. These events are vital to not-for-profits as they seek to acquire resources in support of their mission and also build a sense of community among the supporters of the not-for-profit. These events also create accounting questions surrounding the event including the following:

- Is the event part of the organization's ongoing major or central activities (revenues), or is the event peripheral or incidental to the entity (gains)?
- If membership fees or dues are associated with the event, is the associated revenue stream a contribution or exchange transaction?
- If the event involves the attendee receiving a benefit, (meal, concert, token, and more) is part of the event an exchange transaction?
- How should the costs of putting on the event be treated?

The auditor or accounting professional must exercise professional judgment in distinguishing contributions from exchange transactions. In the technical background for this chapter focuses on determining whether events are part of an organization's ongoing major or central activities and on issues related to membership dues.

## An Important Determination

An important determination in financial reporting for not-for-profits is whether an item is a revenue or expense, a gain or loss. Consider the following differences between expenses and losses:

- *Expenses* are outflows or other using up of assets or incurrences of liabilities (or a combination of both) from delivering or producing goods, rendering services or carrying out other activities that constitute the entity's ongoing major or central operations.
- *Losses* result from activities that are peripheral or incidental to the organization. Activities that are reported as expenses by some organizations may be reported as losses by others. It will depend on whether the activity is part of the organization's ongoing major or central operations.

The determination is important because of the following:

- *There are differences in how expenses and losses are reported.* – Expenses are reported gross,[1] where losses may be reported net.
- *Expenses are always reported as decreases in unrestricted net assets.* – Losses may change other classes of net assets if the use of such losses is restricted by a donor or law.
- *Not-for-profit entities are required to report information about the functional classification of expenses, such as major classes of program services and supporting activities.* – This information can be done on the face of the statement of activities or in the notes to the financial statements. Losses need not be reported by their functional classification or in the matrix that presents information about expenses according to both their functional and natural classifications.

Some activities that are reported as revenues or expenses by some organizations may be reported as gains or losses by others. For example, a girl scout's council could have an annual cookie sale that is its main fundraising event each year (a major and central activity), whereas a boy scouts council could hold a special fundraising cookie sale for new camping equipment that may be considered a peripheral or incidental activity. Both groups are selling cookies, but their reporting of the activity is potentially different.

It may be difficult to determine if an activity is peripheral or incidental to an organization or if the activity is part of the organization's ongoing major or central operations. In making this determination, an organization should consider the frequency of the events and the significance of the event's gross revenue and expenses.

---

[1] The exception to this may be investment related expenses.

## Events Are Considered Ongoing Major and Central if

- they are normally part of an organization's strategy, and the organization normally carries on such activities, or
- the event's gross revenues or expenses are significant in relation to the organization's annual budget.

Events are peripheral or incidental if they are not an integral part of an organization's usual activities or if their gross revenues or expenses are not significant in relation to the organization's annual budget. As stated earlier, revenues and expenses are reported gross; whereas gains and losses may be reported net. In addition, an organization must report information about the functional classification of expenses, but are not required to do so for losses.

## Special Events and Other Fundraising Activities

Many organizations have fundraising or other special events in which the attendee receives some type of direct benefit. For example, an organization may hold a $100 a plate special dinner as a fundraising event. An organization may also hold special social or educational events where the attendee receives a direct benefit. Often, these activities are considered part of the organization's ongoing and major activities and therefore revenues and expenses from such events must be reported.

Organizations have several ways they can report the revenues and expenses from these types of activities. The following is an example of the different ways organizations can report a special fundraising dinner in the statement of activities. Assume the following:

- The price of the dinner is $100.
- The cost of the dinner is $25.
- The fair value of the dinner is $30.
- Additional costs incurred with promoting the dinner is $10.

Now, let us review the possible reporting of this in the following example.

## Three Examples of Reporting a Special Fundraising Dinner

| Example 1 | | | Example 2 | | |
|---|---|---|---|---|---|
| Contributions | | $ 0 | Contributions | | $ 0 |
| Special event revenue | 100 | | Special event revenue | | 100 |
| Less: Cost of direct benefits to donors | (25) | | Total revenue | | 100 |
| Net revenue from special events | | 75 | Cost of direct benefits to donors | | 25 |
| Total contributions and net revenue | | 75 | Fundraising expenses | | 10 |
| Fundraising expenses | | 10 | Total expenses | | 35 |
| Increase in unrestricted net assets | | $ 65 | Increase in unrestricted net assets | | $ 65 |

| Example 3 | | | Important Point |
|---|---|---|---|
| Contributions | | $ 70 | These three examples assume that the special event is part of the organization's ongoing major or central operations and therefore the revenues and expenses from such events are reported gross. If the special event is peripheral or incidental, the organization is permitted to report the activity net of related direct costs. |
| Dinner sales | 30 | | |
| Less: Cost of direct benefits to donors | (25) | | |
| Gross profit on special events | | 5 | |
| Total contributions and net revenue | | 75 | |
| Fundraising expenses | | 10 | |
| Increase in unrestricted net assets | | $ 65 | |

## Membership Dues

Some organizations receive dues from their members. These dues may be considered exchange, part exchange and part contribution or all contribution. Classifying dues depends on tangible or intangible benefits received. For example, if an organization has a membership fee of $100, and the only tangible benefit a member receives is an annual publication with a fair value of $25, the organization would classify $75 of the dues as a contribution and $25 as an exchange transaction. If dues are classified as exchange transactions, they should be recognized as revenue as the earnings process is completed.

Therefore, revenue derived from membership dues in exchange transactions should be recognized over the period to which the dues relate. Nonrefundable initiation and life membership fees received in exchange transactions should be recognized as revenues in the period in which the fees become receivable if future fees are expected to cover the costs of future services to be provided to members. If nonrefundable initiation and life membership fees, rather than future fees, are expected to cover those costs, nonrefundable initiation and life member fees received in exchange transactions should be recognized as revenue over the average duration of membership, the life expectancy of members or other appropriate time periods.

The following, derived from the AICPA *Not-for-Profit Entities* Audit & Accounting Guide, contains a list of indicators from FASB ASC 958 that are helpful in classifying dues. Depending on the facts and circumstances, some indicators may be more significant than others; however, no single indicator is determinative of the classification of a particular transaction.

| | Indicators Useful for Determining the Contribution and Exchange Portions of Membership Dues | |
|---|---|---|
| **Indicator** | **Contribution** | **Exchange Transaction** |
| Recipient not-for-profit's expressed intent concerning purpose of dues payment | The request describes the dues as being used to provide benefits to the general public or to the not-for-profit's service beneficiaries | The request describes the dues as providing economic benefits to members or to other entities or individuals designated by or related to the members |
| Extent of benefits to members | The benefits to members are negligible | The substantive benefits to members (for example, publications, admissions, educational programs, and special events) may be available to nonmembers for a fee |
| Not-for-profit's service efforts | The not-for-profit provides service to members and nonmembers | The not-for-profit benefits are provided only to members |
| Duration of benefits | The duration is not specified | The benefits are provided for a defined period; additional payment of dues is required to extend benefits |

| | Indicators Useful for Determining the Contribution and Exchange Portions of Membership Dues | |
|---|---|---|
| **Indicator** | **Contribution** | **Exchange Transaction** |
| Expressed agreement concerning refundability of the payment | The payment is not refundable to the resource provider | The payment is fully or partially refundable if the resource provider withdraws from membership |
| Qualifications for membership | Membership is available to the general public | Membership is available only to individuals who meet certain criteria (for example, requirements to pursue a specific career or to live in a certain area) |

## KNOWLEDGE CHECK

1. Which is true of indicators that are useful for determining the contribution and exchange portions of membership dues?

    a. Useful indicators exclude the duration of benefits.
    b. Useful indicators exclude the expressed agreement concerning refundability of the payment.
    c. Useful indicators include the qualifications for membership.
    d. Useful indicators exclude extent of benefits.

2. Which is true of indicators that are useful for determining the contribution and exchange portions of membership dues?

    a. A request describing the dues as being used to provide benefits to the general public or to the not-for-profit's service beneficiaries is indicative of an exchange transaction.
    b. Negligible benefits to members is indicative of an exchange transaction.
    c. The not-for-profit providing service to members and nonmembers is indicative of a contribution.
    d. The substantive benefits to members being available to nonmembers for a fee is indicative of a contribution.

3. Which is true of indicators that are useful for determining the contribution and exchange portions of membership dues?

    a. An unspecified duration is indicative of a contribution.

    b. Membership being available to the general public is indicative of an exchange transaction.

    c. Payment is not refundable is an indicator of an exchange transaction.

    d. The benefits are provided for a defined period as indicative of a contribution.

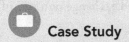

## Case Study

Friends of the New River Theater (FNRT) is a small not-for-profit. Since 2005, the FNRT has operated a not-for-profit movie theater and community center in the heart of the New River Valley. The organization has an annual budget of $80,000.

The organization is governed by a volunteer Board of Directors who serve for three-year terms. The ten member Board is elected by members of the organization. There are currently 340 members. All FNRT members may nominate and vote for new board members at the annual meeting, usually held in May.

Membership is open to the general public. The annual cost of membership is $25 for individuals and $40 for a family. FNRT received $8,200 from membership fees this year. Members receive the following benefits:

- 50 cent discount on all movie tickets
- A newsletter emailed each month
- Advance notice of live events
- Voting rights for board members

This year, FNRT held its first annual formal gala at the theater. The cost to attend the event was $100 and was open to members as well as the general public. Volunteers sent invitations to all members, and an ad was placed in the local paper. The costs of the invitations and ad came to $1,000. A total of 180 people attended the event, and $18,000 was generated from ticket sales. The gala featured live entertainment, local wine, and cheeses. The cost of the event came to $7,200 ($40 per person). It is estimated the event had a fair value of $50 per person. In addition, on the way out of the gala, each attendee was given a key chain with FNRT engraved on one side as a gift for supporting the organization. The costs of the key chains came to $180 ($1 per key chain).

After attending the event, the owner of the large movie theater at the mall offered to sell FNRT their old projection system for $5,000. The system is in good shape and has a fair market value of $15,000. The chair of the FNRT board was thrilled to accept this offer.

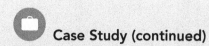

**Case Study (continued)**

Case Study Exercise

Please answer the below questions related to the Friends of the New River Theater.

1. Are the membership fees an exchange transaction or a contribution? Explain.

2. Can FNRT report the net amount from the gala as a gain? Explain.

3. What is the most that FNRT could report as contribution revenue from the gala? Explain.

4. What amount should FNRT report as fundraising expense for the gala event? Explain.

5. Make the journal entry for the purchase of the projection system at a cost of $5,000.

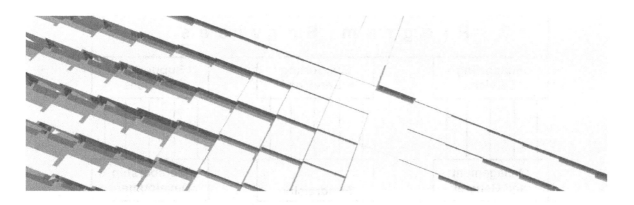

Chapter 12

# ALLOCATION OF COSTS RELATING TO FUNDRAISING

## LEARNING OBJECTIVES

After completing this chapter, you should be able to do the following:

- Determine the essential requirements and decisions connected to the allocation of costs that relate to fundraising.
- Identify characteristics of fundraising activities.

## TECHNICAL BACKGROUND INFORMATION

Not-for-profit entities are required to report information about the functional classification of expenses, such as major classes of program services and supporting activities. This information can be presented in the statement of activities or in the notes to the financial statements.

Program services are activities that result in goods and services being distributed to beneficiaries, customers, or members that fulfill the purposes or mission of the organization. Supporting services are activities other than program services and include management as well as general, fund-raising, and membership development activities. Supporting services may include, as one or more separate categories, cost of sales and costs of other revenue-generating activities that are not program related. The following illustration demonstrates one way of thinking of the relationship between program services and supporting services.

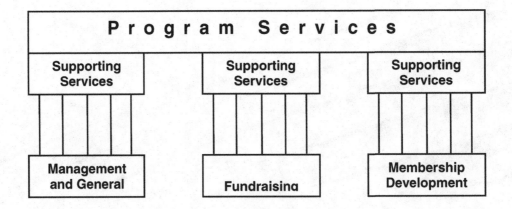

It is imperative that not-for-profit entities classify and report program services and supporting services correctly. Donors and grant providers often compare the percentage of expenses that go to providing program services to the percentage of expenses that go to supporting services. For obvious reasons, the higher the percentage spent on program services, the more favorably resource providers tend to view the not-for-profit. For example, if Not-for-Profit X makes a public appeal for funding to help victims of disaster Y, donors do not like to hear subsequently that a high percentage of the funding that Not-for-Profit X received went to supporting services.

## Program Services

The number of functional reporting classifications for program services varies according to the nature of the services rendered. For some not-for-profits, a single functional reporting classification may be adequate to portray what may, in effect, be a single, integrated program service that the not-for-profit provides. In most cases, however, several separate and identifiable services are provided, and in such cases the expenses for program services should be reported by the kind of service function or group of functions.

FASB ASC 958-720 provides the following examples:

- A large university may have programs for student instruction, research, and patient care, among others.
- A health and welfare entity may have programs for health or family services, research, disaster relief, and public education, among others.

## Supporting Services

Supporting services are often classified as management and general, fundraising, and membership development. However, some not-for-profit industries use other classifications of supporting services. For example, most colleges report institutional support and institutional development activities. Organizations may also report more detailed classifications for each type of supporting services.

### Management and General Activities

Management and general activities are not identifiable with a single program, fundraising activity, or membership development activity, but are essential to the conduct of those activities and to an entity's existence. Examples of management and general activities are illustrated in the following:

Examples of Management and General Activities

- Oversight
- Business management

- General recordkeeping
- Budgeting
- Financing
- Soliciting revenue from exchange transactions
- All management and administration except for direct conduct of program services or fundraising activities

## KNOWLEDGE CHECK

1. Which is true of management and general activities?

    a. Examples of management and general activities include oversight.
    b. Examples of management and general activities exclude business management.
    c. Examples of management and general activities exclude soliciting revenue from exchange transactions.
    d. Examples of management and general activities include soliciting contributions from donors.

The cost of oversight and management usually includes the salaries and expenses of the governing board, the chief executive officer, and the supporting staff. If such staff spend a portion of their time directly supervising program services or categories of other supporting services, however, their salaries and expenses should be allocated among those functions.

## KNOWLEDGE CHECK

2. Which is true of the cost of oversight and management?

    a. The cost of oversight and management usually includes the salaries and expenses of the governing board.
    b. The cost of oversight and management usually excludes the salaries and expenses of the chief executive officer.
    c. The cost of oversight and management usually excludes the salaries and expenses of the supporting staff.
    d. The cost of oversight and management usually includes the salaries and expenses of program managers.

The cost of disseminating information to the public about the "stewardship" of contributed funds, announcements concerning appointments, the annual report, and other similar costs are also included in management and general activities.

### Fundraising Activities

Fundraising activities are connected with inducing potential donors to contribute. The contribution can be money, securities, services, materials, facilities, other assets, or time.

| Fundraising Activities Include |
| --- |
| $     Publicizing and conducting fundraising campaigns |
| $     Maintaining donor mailing lists |
| $     Conducting special fundraising events |
| $     Preparing and distributing fundraising manuals, instructions, and other materials |
| $     Other activities connected with soliciting contributions from individuals, foundations, governments, and others |

The financial statements should disclose total fundraising expenses.

## Membership Development Activities

Membership development activities include soliciting for prospective members and membership dues, membership relations, and similar activities. To the extent that member benefits are received, membership is an exchange transaction. If there are no significant benefits or duties connected with membership, however, the substance of membership development activities may, in fact, be fundraising, and the related costs should be reported as fundraising costs.

Membership development activities may be conducted in conjunction with other activities. In circumstances in which membership development is in part soliciting revenues from exchange transactions and in part soliciting contributions, the activity is a joint activity. If membership development is a joint activity and the purpose, audience, and content of the activity are appropriate for achieving membership development, joint costs should be allocated between fundraising and the exchange transaction. In circumstances in which membership development is conducted in conjunction with other activities but does not include soliciting contributions (for example, the organization's membership dues are entirely exchange transactions, and the activity is in part soliciting new members and in part program activities for existing members), the activity is not a joint activity, and the costs should be allocated to membership development and one or more other functions. For example, membership may entitle the members to group life and other insurance at reduced costs because of the organization's negotiated rates and to a subscription to the organization's magazine or newsletter. Under these circumstances, an appropriate part of the costs of soliciting members should be allocated to the membership development function and a part to program services.

## Classification of Expenses Related to More Than One Function

The correct classification of expenses between program services and supporting activities is often important to not-for-profit entities. Some expenses are easily assigned to a single program or supporting activity. However, some expenses relate to more than one program or supporting activity and must be allocated to the appropriate functions. For example, rent on a building may need to be allocated among program services and supporting activities.

Direct identification of specific expense (also referred to as assigning expenses) is the preferable method of charging expenses to various functions. If an expense can be identified specifically with a program or supporting service, it should be assigned to that function. For example, travel costs incurred in connection with a program activity should be assigned to that program.

Often, it may not be possible or practical to use direct identification to assign costs to various functions. In such cases, an allocation method must be used. Allocating costs is a common practice for both not-for-profit entities and business enterprises. A reasonable allocation of expenses can be made in a variety of ways, and should be based on an objective method if possible. Allocation methods may be based on financial or nonfinancial data. For example, building costs (rent and utilities) may be allocated based on square footage of space occupied by the various programs and support activities. Time records or activity reports may be used to allocate salary of certain personnel. Organizations should review their allocation methods periodically to ensure they reflect the most current activity.

There is special guidance on allocating costs related to an activity that combines fundraising activities and also elements of another function, referred to as *joint activities*.

## Expenses of Materials and Activities Combining Fundraising with Activities Having Elements of another Function (Joint Activities)

Not-for-profit entities may solicit support through a variety of fundraising activities, including, but not limited to, direct mail, telephone solicitation, door-to-door canvassing, telethons, and special events. Sometimes fundraising activities are conducted with activities related to other functions, such as program activities or supporting services, such as management and general activities. Sometimes fundraising activities include components that would otherwise be associated with program or supporting services, but in fact support fundraising.

## KNOWLEDGE CHECK

3. Which is true of fundraising activities?

    a. Not-for-profit entities may solicit support through direct mail.
    b. Not-for-profit entities never solicit support through telephone solicitation.
    c. Not-for-profit entities never solicit support through door-to-door canvassing.
    d. Not-for-profit organizations should include oversight costs in fundraising activities.

```
┌─────────────────────────────────────────────────────────────┐
│         A Key Determination in the Accounting for Joint Activities         │
└─────────────────────────────────────────────────────────────┘
                    │                              │
                    ▼                              ▼
```

| **Allocate** | **Do Not Allocate** |
|---|---|
| If the criteria of purpose, audience, and content are met, the costs of a joint activity identifiable with a particular function should be charged to that function, and joint costs should be allocated between fundraising and the appropriate program or management and general function. | If any of the criteria (purpose, audience, or content) are not met, all costs of the joint activity should be reported as fundraising costs—including costs that otherwise might be considered program or management and general costs if they had been incurred in a different activity. Costs of goods or services provided in exchange transactions that are part of joint activities—such as costs of direct donor benefits of a special event (for example, a meal)—should not be reported as fundraising. |

The following sections, will discuss the purpose, audience, and content criteria.

## Definitions

An understanding of the following definitions is required for this discussion:

- Purpose
- Audience
- Content

### Purpose

The purpose criterion is met if the purpose of the joint activity includes accomplishing program or management and general functions.

#### Program Functions

To accomplish program functions, the activity should call for specific action by the audience that will help accomplish the organization's mission. For example, an organization with a mission to get people to stop smoking may send a brochure that urges the recipient to stop smoking and provides methods to accomplish this task. Conversely, FASB ASC 958-720 provides the following examples of activities that *fail* to call for a specific action by the audience that will help accomplish the not-for-profit's mission:

- Educating the audience about causes or motivating the audience to otherwise engage in specific activities that will educate them about causes is not a call for specific action by the audience that will help accomplish the not-for-profit's mission. Such activities are considered in support of fundraising.
- Asking the audience to make contributions is not a call for specific action by the audience that will help accomplish the not-for-profit's mission.

The following factors should be considered (in the order listed) to determine if the purpose criterion is met:

- *The compensation or fees test* – The purpose criterion is not met if a majority of compensation or fees for any party's performance of any component of the discrete joint activity varies based on contributions raised for that discrete joint activity.
- *The separate and similar activities test* – [Note: If the purpose criterion is met based on the *separate and similar activities test*, the *other evidence test* (discussed as follows) should not be considered.] The purpose criterion is met if either of the following two conditions is met:
    - *Condition 1* – The program component of the joint activity calls for specific action by the recipient that will help accomplish the organization's mission and a similar program component is conducted without the fundraising component using the same medium and on a scale that is similar to or greater than the scale on which it is conducted with the fundraising.
    - *Condition 2* – A management and general activity that is similar to the management and general component of the joint activity being accounted for is conducted without the fundraising component using the same medium and on a scale that is similar to or greater than the scale on which it is conducted with the fundraising.

- *The other evidence test* – If the preceding factors do not determine whether the purpose criterion is met, other evidence may determine whether the criterion is met. All available evidence, both positive and negative, should be considered to determine whether, based on the weight of that evidence, the purpose criterion is met.

## Audience

A rebuttable presumption exists that the audience criterion is not met if the audience includes prior donors or is otherwise selected based on its ability or likelihood to contribute to the organization. That presumption can be overcome if the audience is also selected for one or more of the following reasons. In determining whether that presumption is overcome, organizations should consider the extent to which the audience is selected based on its ability or likelihood to contribute to the organization and contrast that with the extent to which it is selected for one or more of the following reasons. For example, if the audience's ability or likelihood to contribute is a significant factor in its selection, and it has a need for the action related to the program component of the joint activity, but having that need is an insignificant factor in its selection, the presumption would not be overcome.

In circumstances in which the audience includes no prior donors and is not otherwise selected based on its ability or likelihood to contribute to the organization, the audience criterion is met if the audience is selected for one or more of the following reasons:

- The audience's need to use or reasonable potential for use of the specific action called for by the program component of the joint activity.
- The audience's ability to take specific action to assist the organization in meeting the goals of the program component of the joint activity.
- The organization is required to direct the management and general component of the joint activity to the particular audience or the audience has reasonable potential for use of the management and general component.

## Content

The content criterion is met if the joint activity supports program or management and general functions, as follows:

- *Program* – The joint activity calls for specific action by the recipient that will help accomplish the organization's mission. If the need for and benefits of the action are not clearly evident, information describing the action and explaining the need for and benefits of the action is provided.
- *Management and general* – The joint activity fulfills one or more of the organization's management and general responsibilities through a component of the joint activity.

Information identifying and describing the organization, its causes, or how the contributions provided will be used is considered in support of fundraising.

## Allocation Methods

The cost allocation methodology used should be rational and systematic, should result in an allocation of joint costs that is reasonable, and should be applied consistently given similar facts and circumstances.

## Disclosures

As illustrated in the following, not-for-profits that allocate joint costs have several disclosure requirements:

| Not-for-Profits that Allocate Joint Costs Should Disclose the Following in the Notes to the Financial Statements: |
| --- |
| The types of activities for which joint costs have been incurred. |
| A statement that such costs have been allocated. |
| The total amount allocated during the period and the portion allocated to each functional expense category. |

Organizations are encouraged, but not required, to disclose the amount of joint costs for each kind of joint activity, if practical.

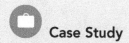 **Case Study**

Review the following situations and answer the questions presented.

**Situation 1**

Not-for-Profit A's mission is to improve the quality of life for senior citizens. One of Not-for-Profit A's objectives included in that mission is to increase the physical activity of senior citizens. One of Not-for-Profit A's programs to attain that objective is to send representatives to speak to groups about the importance of exercise and to conduct exercise classes.

Not-for-Profit A mails a brochure on the importance of exercise that encourages exercise in later years to residents over the age of 65 in three ZIP code areas. The last two pages of the four-page brochure include a perforated contribution remittance form on which Not-for-Profit A explains its program and makes an appeal for contributions. The content of the first two pages of the brochure is primarily educational; it explains how seniors can undertake a self-supervised exercise program and encourages them to undertake such a program. In addition, Not-for-Profit A includes a second brochure on various exercise techniques that can be used by those undertaking an exercise program.

The brochures are distributed to educate people in this age group about the importance of exercising, to help them exercise properly, and to raise contributions for Not-for-Profit A. These objectives are documented in a letter to the public relations firm that developed the brochures. The audience is selected based on age, without regard to ability to contribute. Not-for-Profit A believes that most of the recipients would benefit from the information about exercise.

1.   Should the joint costs related to the brochure be allocated? If so, why?

2.   If Not-for-profit A had employed a fundraising consultant to develop the first brochure and paid that consultant 30 percent of contributions raised, would that change your answer?

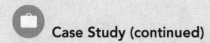 **Case Study (continued)**

### Situation 2

Not-for-Profit C's mission is to provide summer camps for economically disadvantaged youths. Educating the families of ineligible youths about the camps is not one of the program objectives included in that mission.

Not-for-Profit C conducts a door-to-door solicitation campaign for its camp programs. In the campaign, volunteers with canisters visit homes in middle-class neighborhoods to collect contributions. Not-for-Profit C believes that people in those neighborhoods would not need the camp's programs but may contribute. The volunteers explain the camp's programs, including why the disadvantaged children benefit from the program, and distribute leaflets to the residents regardless of whether they contribute to the camp. The leaflets describe the camp, its activities, who can attend, and the benefits to attendees. Requests for contributions are not included in the leaflets.

Should the joint costs of conducting the campaign be allocated? If so, why?

### Situation 3

Not-for-profit D is a university that distributes its annual report, which includes reports on mission accomplishments, to those who have made significant contributions over the previous year, its board of trustees, and its employees. The annual report is primarily prepared by management and general personnel, such as the accounting department and executive staff. The activity is coordinated by the public relations department. Internal management memoranda indicate that the purpose of the annual report is to report on how management discharged its stewardship responsibilities, including the university's overall performance, goals, financial position, cash flows, and results of operations. Included in the package containing the annual report are requests for contributions and donor reply cards.

Should the joint costs of distributing the annual report be allocated? If so, why?

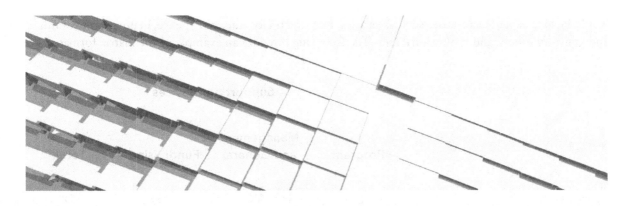

Chapter 13

# AUDIT ISSUES RELATED TO THE STATEMENT OF FUNCTIONAL EXPENSES

## LEARNING OBJECTIVES

After completing this chapter, you should be able to do the following:

- Determine which organizations are required to include a statement of functional expenses.
- Identify risks related to the statement of functional expenses.
- Identify audit procedures to address identified risks related to the statement of functional expenses.
- Identify audit considerations related to management's estimates.

## TECHNICAL BACKGROUND INFORMATION

A statement of activities or the notes to the financial statements should provide information about expenses reported by their functional classification, such as major classes of program services and supporting activities. FASB ASC 958-720, *Not-for-Profit Entities – Other Expenses*, provides guidance for presenting a statement of functional expenses, which is useful in associating expenses with service efforts and accomplishments. Voluntary health and welfare entities should report information about expenses by their functional classes—defined as major classes of program or management and general services or fundraising services and supporting activities—together with information about expenses by their natural classification in a matrix format in a standalone financial statement. A natural classification of expenses would include expense categories such as salaries, rent, electricity, interest expense, depreciation, awards and grants to others, and professional fees. The following provides an example of the matrix format:

|  | | Supporting Services | | |
| --- | --- | --- | --- | --- |
|  | Program | Management and General | Fundraising | Total |
| Salaries | $X | $X | $X | $X |
| Rent | X | X | X | X |
| Electricity | X | X | X | X |
| Interest expense | X | X | X | X |
| Depreciation | X | X | X | X |
| Awards and grants to others | X | X | X | X |
| Professional fees | X | X | X | X |
| Total expenses | $X | $X | $X | $X |

To the extent that expenses are reported by other than their natural classification (such as salaries included in cost of goods sold or facility rental costs of special events reported as direct benefits to donors), they should be reported by their natural classification if a statement of functional expenses is presented. For example, salaries, wages, and fringe benefits that are included as part of the cost of goods sold on the statement of activities should be included with other salaries, wages, and fringe benefits in the statement of functional expenses. In addition, expenses that are netted against investment revenues should be reported by their functional classification on the statement of functional expenses (if the not-for-profit presents that statement). Other not-for-profits, such as non-voluntary health and welfare organizations, are encouraged, but not required, to provide information about expenses by their natural expense classification.

## KNOWLEDGE CHECK

1.  Which is NOT true of a natural classification of expenses?

    a.  A natural classification of expenses would include expense categories such as fundraising expenses.
    b.  A natural classification of expenses would include expense categories such as rent.
    c.  A natural classification of expenses would include expense categories such as professional fees.
    d.  A natural classification of expenses would include expense categories such as salaries.

## Auditor Considerations

There are a variety of issues the auditor must consider before expressing an opinion on the fair presentation of the statement of functional expenses. Some of these considerations are illustrated as follows:

- The risk of fraudulent financial reporting of the functional classification of expenses
- The risk of material misstatement in classification due to error
- The challenge of auditing management's estimates inherent to the statement of functional expenses
- The challenge of auditing complex calculations
- Designing audit procedures to provide sufficient, appropriate evidence regarding the fair presentation of the statement of functional expenses

Functional classification refers to the major classes of program services and of supporting activities, such as fundraising activities, membership development activities, and management and general activities. Natural classification refers to the kinds of expenses incurred, such as salaries and wages, utilities, and professional services.

Organizations receiving grants or donations from other organizations often are evaluated on the information provided by the statement of functional expenses. Donors or granting agencies may consider the percent of resources expended on program services or management and general activities. They may also consider the amount of resources expended on fundraising activities as a percentage of donations received. The statement of functional expenses provides information regarding resources expended on organization personnel, facilities, professional fees, and other areas. Donors and granting agencies that have access to this information often make funding decisions based on it. This can make the information reported on the statement of functional expenses critical to the ongoing activities of an organization.

The statement of functional expenses can be the most important financial statement to the users of the financial statements, providing incentive for the information to be misstated. This should be part of the auditor's consideration of fraud risk factors. As part of the audit, the auditor assesses risk of material misstatement by assertion. For many organizations, the risk of material misstatement for the classification assertion will be assessed at high. The auditor will also consider whether substantive procedures can provide sufficient, appropriate evidence regarding the fair presentation of the classification of expenses. If substantive procedures alone cannot provide sufficient, appropriate evidence, the auditor must test controls over classification of expenses.

Audit procedures to address classification of expenses presented in the statement of functional expenses will be unique to each auditee. The natural types of expenses incurred, and the method by which the organization classifies the functional expenses, will be unique to each organization. Some costs are directly identifiable to a particular function, but many costs are allocated between more than one function. The method of allocation will vary based on the type of cost. Often, each natural classification contains expenses that were allocated using different methods (such as according to full-time equivalent or, according to square footage).

## Knowledge Check

2.  Which is typically true of auditor considerations related to the statement of functional expenses?

    a.  The risk of fraudulent financial reporting of the natural classification of expenses is a consideration.
    b.  The risk of material misstatement in completeness due to error is a consideration.
    c.  The challenge of auditing estimates by management inherent to the statement of functional expenses is a consideration.
    d.  The challenge of auditing immaterial account balances is a consideration.

Consider the natural classification of professional fees as an example. Professional fees may consist of legal services, audit fees, clinician services, workplace design services, and computer support. Management may determine that legal services and audit fees are directly identified as management and general activities. Management may determine that clinician services are identified directly as program services. Workplace design services may be allocated to functional classification based on square footage used for program services, management and general activities, and fundraising activities. Computer support may be allocated to functional classification based on percentage of computers used for program services, management and general activities, and fundraising activities. Testing the natural and functional classification of professional services could involve the following:

- Reviewing supporting invoices for all professional services for occurrence, accuracy, cutoff, and natural classification.
- Reviewing supporting invoices for legal services, audit fees, and clinician services for functional classification.
- Determining total square footage of facilities affected by workplace design services.
- Determining square footage used by program services, management and general activities, and fundraising activities.
- Determining the allocation of workplace design services is appropriate.
- Determining total number of computers used. Also determining the number of computers used by program services, management and general activities, and fundraising activities.
- Determining the allocation of computer support as appropriate.

The determination of square footage and computers used by program services, management and general activities, and fundraising activities will most likely involve evaluating estimates by management.

### Is This Estimate on Target?

Estimates by their very nature include a degree of uncertainty. The degree of uncertainty affects the risk of material misstatement. Estimates may be susceptible to management bias (or, potentially, an increased likelihood of fraud, given a certain level of incentive).

Auditing management's estimates include identifying significant assumptions used by management and determining that they are reasonable. Auditing management's estimates also includes evaluating the information used to make those estimates. For example, if management estimates that 10 percent of the executive director's time is spent on fundraising activities, the auditor would evaluate information supporting that estimate. Such information could include time sheets, board minutes, appointment calendar, inquiry of other personnel, and other information the auditor deems useful.

We have discussed that the functional classification of expenses may involve more than one allocation method, even within one natural expense category. An example is that payroll may include expenses that were directly identified with functional classifications (program personnel, accounts payable clerk, and more.) Payroll may also include expenses that were allocated based on time spent as recorded on a time sheet or allocated based on estimated time spent. Another example is that computer support may be allocated to functional classification based on full-time equivalents charged to program services, management and general activities, and fundraising activities.

Testing these allocations involves testing each part of the calculation. If computer support is allocated to functional classification based on full-time equivalents charged to program services, management and general activities, and fundraising activities, the auditor would need to test the following items: (*a*) total full-time equivalents for the organization; (*b*) full-time equivalents for program services, management and general activities, and fundraising activities; (*c*) total computer support expense; and (*d*) the allocation of computer support expense to each functional classification.

Such tests can involve a great deal of time by the auditor. Because the statement of functional expenses may involve the most significant estimates by management, and because the statement of functional expenses may present the greatest risk for fraudulent financial reporting, the auditor should consider their audit procedures carefully to address these risks and to obtain sufficient, appropriate evidence to support their opinion on the fair presentation of the statement of functional expenses.

## KNOWLEDGE CHECK

3. Which is typically NOT true of testing the natural and functional classification of professional services?

   a. Testing could involve reviewing supporting invoices for all professional services for occurrence, accuracy, cutoff, and natural classification.
   b. Testing could involve comparing total expenses by functional classification with other organizations.
   c. Testing could involve reviewing supporting invoices for legal services, audit fees, and clinician services for functional classification.
   d. Testing could involve determining total square footage of facilities affected by workplace design services.

Performing analytical procedures can provide the auditor with useful information. An important and integral part of performing analytical procedures is for the auditor to have developed expectations for those analytical procedures. Comparison to the prior year is a common procedure. However, it is unusual that an organization will have had no change in its programs, processes, personnel, or activities from one year to the next. Comparison to the prior year can be helpful, but the auditor should include consideration of expected changes in the current year. The auditor's understanding of the organization, including the industry and economic factors that affect its activities, will need to be considered in developing those expectations. For example, was there a cost of living increase to salaries? Was there a change to health insurance or other employee benefits? Was there a change in travel costs or mileage reimbursement? Was there a change in utility rates? Was there a change to business insurance costs? One of the traps of comparison to the prior year is that if there was fraud in the prior year (either due to fraudulent financial reporting or misappropriation of assets), comparison to the prior year will most likely not reveal that fraud to the auditor.

## The Uniqueness of Not-for-Profits

Comparison to other not-for-profit entities may not be as helpful as comparing similar for-profit companies. Not-for-profit entities are diverse in their missions, structures, programs, and activities. Comparison to expectations developed based on review of agreements, invoices, and other documents may be a valuable procedure to the auditor to provide evidence as to particular assertions for a class of transactions or an account balance.

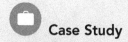

## Case Study

### Situation 1

Not-for-Profit Z provides medical services for homeless and displaced children. Not-for-Profit Z receives more than 80 percent of its funding from foundations and individuals in the form of donations. The remaining revenue consists of program service fees and other revenues. There is a lot of competition for these funds. Part of the funding received is based on Not-for-Profit Z's ability to match those funds with in-kind donations of medical services and medical equipment. The following is the statement of functional expenses for the year ended December 31, 20X3.

|  | Program Services | Management and General | Fundraising | Total |
|---|---|---|---|---|
| Payroll | 948,000 | 105,000 | 47,000 | 1,100,000 |
| Payroll taxes and employee benefits | 213,000 | 5,000 | 2,000 | 220,000 |
| Professional services – medical | 200,000 | | | 200,000 |
| Professional services – other | 127,000 | 23,000 | | 150,000 |
| Supplies and equipment | 100,000 | 19,000 | 1,000 | 120,000 |
| Occupancy | 72,000 | 8,000 | | 80,000 |
| Insurance | 45,000 | 5,000 | | 50,000 |
| Training and development | 45,000 | 5,000 | | 50,000 |
| Other | 20,000 | 10,000 | | 30,000 |
| Total | 1,770,000 | 180,000 | 50,000 | 2,000,000 |

1. Is Not-for-Profit Z required to present a statement of functional expenses? Explain your answer.

2. You are a member of the audit team and participating in the brainstorming session. What risk factors do you identify related to the statement of functional expenses?

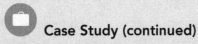 **Case Study (continued)**

3. Upon what areas would you focus the audit team's procedures regarding the statement of functional expenses?

### Situation 2

Let us presume a different set of facts. Instead of receiving more than 80 percent of its funding from foundations and individuals, Not-for-Profit Z receives its revenue in the form of program service fees. The organization does not pursue donations as they perceive it to be a lot of work for little benefit. The following is the statement of functional expenses for the year ended December 31, 20X3.

|  | Program Services | Management and General | Total |
|---|---|---|---|
| Payroll | 986,000 | 114,000 | 1,100,000 |
| Payroll taxes and employee benefits | 215,000 | 5,000 | 220,000 |
| Professional services – medical | 200,000 |  | 200,000 |
| Professional services – other | 127,000 | 23,000 | 150,000 |
| Supplies and equipment | 100,000 | 20,000 | 120,000 |
| Occupancy | 72,000 | 8,000 | 80,000 |
| Insurance | 45,000 | 5,000 | 50,000 |
| Training and development | 45,000 | 5,000 | 50,000 |
| Other | 20,000 | 10,000 | 30,000 |
| Total | 1,810,000 | 190,000 | 2,000,000 |

1. Is Not-for-Profit Z required to present a statement of functional expenses? Explain your answer.

2. You are a member of the audit team and participating in the brainstorming session. What risk factors do you identify related to the statement of functional expenses?

3. Upon what areas would you focus the audit team's procedures regarding the statement of functional expenses?

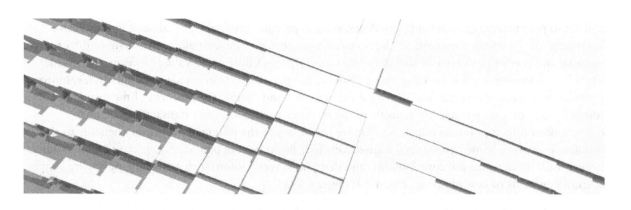

# Chapter 14

# NAMING RIGHTS

## LEARNING OBJECTIVES

After completing this chapter, you should be able to do the following:

- Apply your understanding of unrelated business income tax issues.

## TECHNICAL BACKGROUND INFORMATION

Some not-for-profit entities (NFPs) offer public recognition, such as what are sometimes referred to as naming opportunities, and other rights and privileges to resource providers. For example, an NFP may give resource providers the opportunity to name a building or a portion thereof, based on receiving certain dollar amounts. Alternatively, a college or university may give resource providers the opportunity to name a faculty position and have certain recruiting privileges, based on receiving certain dollar amounts.

FASB defines a contribution as "An unconditional transfer of cash or other assets to an entity or a settlement or cancellation of its liabilities in a voluntary nonreciprocal transfer by entity acting other than as an owner. Other assets include securities, land, buildings, use of facilities or utilities, materials and supplies, intangible assets, and unconditional promises to give those items in the future." Some exchange transactions may appear to be much like contributions; therefore, a careful assessment of the characteristics of the transaction is required to determine whether the recipient of a transfer of assets has given up an asset or incurred a liability of commensurate value.

The board believes that assessing the characteristics of transactions from the perspectives of both the resource provider and the recipient is necessary to determine whether a contribution has occurred. For example, a resource provider may sponsor research and development activities at a research university and retain proprietary rights or other privileges, such as patents, copyrights, or advance and exclusive knowledge of the research outcomes. The research outcomes may be intangible, uncertain, or difficult to measure and may be perceived by the university as a sacrifice of little or no value; however, their value often is commensurate with the value that a resource provider expects in exchange. Similarly, a resource provider may sponsor research and development activities and specify the protocol of the testing so the research outcomes are particularly valuable to the resource provider. Those transactions are not contributions if their potential public benefits are secondary to the potential proprietary benefits to the resource providers. Some believe such transactions may be, at least in part, exchange transactions. Others believe such transactions are contributions, and that public recognition, such as naming rights, are simply acknowledgments of contributions. Practice is diverse.

However, in some cases, such public recognition and other rights and privileges do not result in significant value to the resource provider, and therefore should be reported as contributions. NFPs should consider whether in fact such transactions are contributions, exchange transactions, or some combination of both. NFPs should consider the specific facts and circumstances of such public recognition and other rights and privileges, such as the type of resource provider (individual or corporation), rights and benefits transferred, contract stipulations, length of time that the benefit is provided, and control over name and logo use.

In determining the fair value, if any, of the public recognition and other rights and privileges, NFPs should apply the guidance in FASB *Fair Value Measurements*. Factors that may be relevant in determining fair value pursuant to FASB include, but are not limited to, the contractual stipulations or independent appraisals. If a combination of both contribution and exchange transaction is present, the NFP should unbundle the transaction and determine the fair value of the contribution and exchange transaction components. The NFP should consider stipulations placed on the use of the resources provided, if any, in determining the nature of the contribution portion received (for example, unrestricted or restricted). Revenues received from the exchange transaction component should be recorded consistent with exchange transaction recognition principles. In some instances, if there are multiple "deliverables" spanning a period of years as part of the exchange transaction, it is possible that the contribution element would be reflected in current year's revenues, but some or all portions of the exchange transaction components could be deferred.

## KNOWLEDGE CHECK

1. If a combination of both contribution and exchange transaction is present, the NFP should

    a. Unbundle the transaction and determine the fair value of the contribution and exchange transaction components.

    b. Record the transaction as a contribution.

    c. Record the transaction as an exchange.

    d. Record the transaction as miscellaneous revenue.

2. In accounting for not-for-profit entities, revenues received from the exchange transaction component of a transaction should

     a. Follow guidance different from exchange transaction recognition principles.

     b. Be recorded consistent with exchange transaction recognition principles.

     c. Never be recognized on a deferred basis.

     d. Not be recorded in a not-for-profits financial statements.

## Unrelated Business Income

Unrelated business income is the income from a trade or business that is conducted regularly by an exempt organization and that is not substantially related to the performance by the organization of its exempt purpose or function, except that the organization uses the profits derived from this activity.

### Trade or Business

The term "trade or business" generally includes any activity carried on for the production of income from selling goods or performing services. An activity does not lose its identity as a trade or business merely because it is carried on within a larger group of similar activities that may be related to the exempt purposes of the organization.

For example, the regular sale of pharmaceutical supplies to the general public by a hospital pharmacy does not lose its identity as a trade or business, even though the pharmacy also furnishes supplies to the hospital and patients of the hospital in accordance with its exempt purpose. Similarly, soliciting, selling, and publishing commercial advertising is a trade or business even though the advertising is published in an exempt organization's periodical that contains editorial matter related to the organization's exempt purpose.

### Regularly Carried On

Business activities of an exempt organization ordinarily are considered regularly carried on if they show a frequency and continuity and are pursued in a manner similar to comparable commercial activities of nonexempt organizations.

For example, a hospital auxiliary's operation of a sandwich stand for two weeks at a state fair would not be the regular conduct of a trade or business. The stand would not compete with similar facilities that a nonexempt organization ordinarily would operate year-round. However, operating a commercial parking lot every Saturday, year-round, would be the regular conduct of a trade or business.

### Not Substantially Related

A business activity is not substantially related to an organization's exempt purpose if it does not contribute importantly to accomplishing that purpose, other than through the production of funds. Whether an activity contributes importantly depends in each case on the facts involved.

In determining whether activities contribute importantly to the accomplishment of an exempt purpose, the size and extent of the activities involved must be considered in relation to the nature and extent of the exempt function that they intend to serve. For example, to the extent an activity is conducted on a scale larger than is reasonably necessary to perform an exempt purpose, it does not contribute importantly to the accomplishment of the exempt purpose. The part of the activity deemed more than needed to accomplish the exempt purpose is an unrelated trade or business.

Following is more information about the three principles applied in the determination of whether an activity contributes to the accomplishment of an exempt purpose, and therefore whether it is not substantially related.

### Exploitation of Exempt Functions

Exempt activities sometimes create goodwill or other intangibles that can be exploited in a commercial way. When an organization exploits such an intangible in commercial activities, the fact that the income depends in part upon an exempt function of the organization does not make the commercial activities a related trade or business. Unless the commercial exploitation contributes importantly to the accomplishment of the exempt purpose, the commercial activities are an unrelated trade or business.

### Selling of Products of Exempt Functions

Ordinarily, selling products that result from the performance of exempt functions is not an unrelated trade or business if the product is sold in substantially the same state it is in when the exempt functions are completed. Thus, for an exempt organization engaged in rehabilitating handicapped persons (its exempt function), selling articles made by these persons as part of their rehabilitation training is not an unrelated trade or business.

However, if a completed product resulting from an exempt function is used or exploited in further business activity beyond what is reasonably appropriate or necessary to dispose of it as is, the activity is an unrelated trade or business. For example, if an exempt organization maintains an experimental dairy herd for scientific purposes, the sale of milk and cream produced in the ordinary course of operation of the project is not an unrelated trade or business. However, if the organization uses the milk and cream in the further manufacture of food items such as ice cream, pastries, and more, the sale of these products is an unrelated trade or business unless the manufacturing activities themselves contribute importantly to the accomplishment of an exempt purpose of the organization.

### Dual Use of Assets or Facilities

If an asset or facility necessary to the conduct of exempt functions is also used in commercial activities, its use for exempt functions does not, by itself, make the commercial activities a related trade or business. The test, as discussed earlier, is whether the activities contribute importantly to the accomplishment of exempt purposes.

For example, a museum has a theater auditorium designed for showing educational films in connection with its program of public education in the arts and sciences. The theater is a principal feature of the museum and operates continuously while the museum is open to the public. If the organization also operates the theater as a motion picture theater for the public when the museum is closed, the activity is an unrelated trade or business.

### Excluded Trade or Business Activities

The following activities are specifically excluded from the definition of unrelated trade or business.

#### Qualified Sponsorship Activities

Soliciting and receiving qualified sponsorship payments is not an unrelated trade or business, and the payments are not subject to unrelated business income tax.

#### Qualified Sponsorship Payment

This is any payment made by a person engaged in a trade or business for which the person will receive no substantial benefit other than the use or acknowledgment of the business name, logo, or product lines in connection with the organization's activities. The organization's activities include all its activities, whether or not related to its exempt purposes. For example, if, in return for receiving a sponsorship payment, an organization promises to use the sponsor's name or logo in acknowledging the sponsor's support for an educational or fundraising event, the payment is a qualified sponsorship payment and is not subject to the unrelated business income tax.

Providing facilities, services, or other privileges (for example, complimentary tickets, pro-am playing spots in golf tournaments, or receptions for major donors) to a sponsor or the sponsor's designees in connection with a sponsorship payment does not affect whether the payment is a qualified sponsorship payment. Instead, providing these goods or services is treated as a separate transaction in determining whether the organization has unrelated business income from the event. Generally, if the services or facilities are not a substantial benefit or if providing them is a related business activity, the payments will not be subject to the unrelated business income tax.

Similarly, the sponsor's receipt of a license to use an intangible asset (for example, a trademark, logo, or designation) of the organization is treated as separate from the qualified sponsorship transaction in determining whether the organization has unrelated business taxable income.

If part of a payment would be a qualified sponsorship payment if paid separately, that part is treated as a separate payment. For example, if a sponsorship payment entitles the sponsor to both product advertising and the use or acknowledgment of the sponsor's name or logo by the organization, then the unrelated business income tax does not apply to the part of the payment that is more than the fair market value of the product advertising.

## Qualified Sponsorship Payment Exceptions

There are certain transactions that are not considered to be a qualified sponsorship payment. Following are four payments exceptions, with an explanation as to why they do not qualify:

### Advertising

A payment is not a qualified sponsorship payment if, in return, the organization advertises the sponsor's products or services.

Advertising includes

- messages containing qualitative or comparative language, price information, or other indications of savings or value:
- endorsements: and
- inducements to purchase, sell, or use the products or services.

The use of promotional logos or slogans that are an established part of the sponsor's identity is not, by itself, advertising. In addition, mere distribution or display of a sponsor's product by the organization to the public at a sponsored event, whether for free or for remuneration, is considered use or acknowledgment of the product rather than advertising.

### Exception for Contingent Payments

A payment is not a qualified sponsorship payment if its amount is contingent, by contract or otherwise, upon the level of attendance at one or more events, broadcast ratings, or other factors indicating the degree of public exposure to one or more events. However, the fact that a sponsorship payment is contingent upon an event actually taking place or being broadcast does not, by itself, affect whether a payment qualifies.

### Exception for Periodicals

A payment is not a qualified sponsorship payment if it entitles the payer to the use or acknowledgment of the business name, logo, or product lines in the organization's periodical. For this purpose, a periodical is any regularly scheduled and printed material (for example, a monthly journal) published by or on behalf of the organization. It does not include material that is related to and primarily distributed in connection with a specific event conducted by the organization (for example, a program or brochure distributed at a sponsored event).

### Exception for Conventions and Trade Shows

A payment is not a qualified sponsorship payment if it is made in connection with any qualified convention or trade show activity.

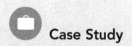

## Case Study

The executive director of College A is approached by Nika Sporting Goods' chairman of the board, Mr. Eyeneeda, who graduated from College A some 30 years ago and has never contributed to the institution. Nika Sporting Goods is an international entity that develops, manufactures, and sells athletic equipment and clothing for all international and national sports. He indicates that his company is interested in making a contribution to the new Athletic Building provided the building will be named the Nika Athletic Facility. The Executive Director informs Mr. Eyeneeda that he has procured all the funds necessary to build the facility, and it looks like it will be named the "Widget Makers Athletic Complex" because they committed $2,500,000 toward the construction.

However, they do need a new football stadium in order to continue conducting their annual New Year's Day Bowl game for the TRUE National Championship for collegiate football. They have launched this endeavor to attract undefeated Division 1 teams that are being shunned by the tainted media voters. They have run bowl games for the past three years with limited success. However, they were just awarded a contract by HGTV for exclusive broadcast rights on New Year's Day for the next 5 years to supplement the Channel's annual non-commercial telecast of the Rose Bowl Parade. If the ratings are good enough, HGTV has indicated that they would be willing to make the agreement extend for another 20 years. However, attracting the top two undefeated teams that have been snubbed has been a problem because they have no funds to give the institutions to defray their costs. The Executive Director is concerned that HGTV will renege on their commitment if the college cannot attract the intended teams. Mr. Eyeneeda indicates that he will be back to the Executive Director within the next week.

The following week, the Executive Director is informed by Mr. Eyeneeda of the following:

- Nika Sporting Goods will build a new stadium for the college that will seat 100,000 fans. The company's architect and general contractor estimate that the stadium will cost approximately $75,000,000.
- The stadium will be called the "Nika Athletic Stadium" and will have the corporate logo displayed in each end zone and on the press box and luxury boxes.
- The New Year's Day game will be called the "Nika National Championship Bowl Game".
- This agreement to naming rights shall be contractually agreed to by the college and the company for a period of 25 years with an option to retain the naming rights for another 25 years for a payment of $10,000,000 at the conclusion of the first 25 year period.
- In the event of a name change by the company through either a merger or acquisition, then the college will make the necessary name and logo changes at the cost of the company to both the stadium and the bowl game.
- The college will receive a yearly contribution of $500,000 to assist in defraying the cost of running the bowl game and each team's institution will receive $3,000,000 each for playing in the game.

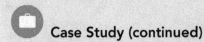

## Case Study (continued)

Based on the facts given and the technical background information:

1. Do you believe the institution has received any contributions within this setup by Mr. Eyeneeda, or is there any exchange value for entering into this agreement for the Nika Sporting Goods Company?

2. Do the IRS rules for Unrelated Business Income matter within this context? That is, if it is UBI, then it has to be an exchange transaction, or, if it is not UBI, then it has to be a contribution.

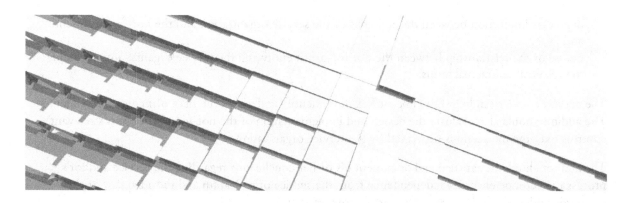

# Chapter 15

# RECENT ISSUES

## LEARNING OBJECTIVES

After you have completed this chapter, you should be able to do the following:

- Identify issues regarding transactions processed by service organizations.
- Identify accounting requirements for programmatic investments.
- Recognize when guidance for group audits may apply.

## TECHNICAL BACKGROUND INFORMATION – TRANSACTIONS PROCESSED BY SERVICE ORGANIZATIONS

Not-for-profit entities may use service organizations to process their transactions. Common examples of transactions processed by service organizations are payroll, investment management services, student financial aid payments, and receipts of contributions. Management should design internal control to include these transactions.

Auditors of not-for-profit entities, also referred to as **user auditors**, should obtain an understanding of how the not-for-profit entity, also referred to as the **user entity**, uses the services of the service organization. The auditor's documentation of their understanding should address the

- nature of the services provided by the service organization and the significance of those services to the not-for-profit entity, including their effect on the not-for-profit entity's internal control;
- nature and materiality of the transactions processed or accounts or financial reporting processes affected by the service organization;

- degree of interaction between the activities of the service organization and the not-for-profit entity; and
- nature of the relationship between the not-for-profit entity and the service organization, including the relevant contractual terms.

The auditor's understanding should be sufficient to identify and assess the risks of material misstatement. The auditor should also evaluate the design and implementation of the not-for-profit entity's relevant controls over the transactions processed by the service organization.

The auditor should be satisfied and document his or her conclusions regarding the service auditor's professional competence and independence from the service organization and the adequacy of the standards under which the service auditor's report was issued.

The auditor should inquire of management about whether the service organization has reported to the not-for-profit entity (or if management is otherwise aware of) any fraud, noncompliance with laws and regulations, or uncorrected misstatements affecting the financial statements. The auditor should evaluate how such matters, if any, affect the nature, timing, and extent of the audit procedures to be performed. The auditor should also evaluate how such matters affect the auditor's conclusions and the auditor's report.

## Using the Service Auditor's Report

If the auditor plans to use the service auditor's report as audit evidence to support the auditor's *understanding* about the design and implementation of controls at the service organization, the auditor should perform the following procedures:

- Evaluate whether the report is as of a date or is for a period that is appropriate for the auditor's purposes.
- Evaluate the sufficiency and appropriateness of the evidence provided by the report for the understanding of the not-for-profit entity's internal control relevant to the audit.
- Determine whether complementary controls identified by the service organization are relevant in addressing the risks of material misstatement relating to the relevant assertions in the not-for-profit entity's financial statements. If the complementary controls are relevant, the auditor should obtain an understanding of whether the not-for-profit entity has designed and implemented such controls.

If the auditor plans to use a type 2 report as audit evidence [which describes] *that controls at the service organization are operating effectively*, the auditor should determine whether the service auditor's report provides sufficient appropriate audit evidence about the effectiveness of the controls to support the auditor's risk assessment. To do this, the auditor should perform the following procedures:

- Evaluate whether the type 2 report is for a period that is appropriate for the auditor's purposes.
- Determine whether complementary controls identified by the service organization are relevant in addressing the risks of material misstatement relating to the relevant assertions in the not-for-profit entity's financial statements. If complimentary controls are relevant, the auditor should obtain an understanding of whether the not-for-profit entity has designed and implemented such controls. If the not-for-profit entity has implemented such controls, the auditor should test their operating effectiveness.
- Evaluate the adequacy of the time period covered by the tests of controls and the time elapsed since the performance of the tests of controls.
- Evaluate whether the tests of controls performed by the service auditor and the results thereof, as described in the service auditor's report, are relevant to the assertions in the not-for-profit entity's financial statements and provide sufficient appropriate audit evidence to support the auditor's risk assessment.

## KNOWLEDGE CHECK

1. Which is a required audit procedure regarding service organizations?

    a. The auditor should be satisfied regarding the service auditor's professional competence and independence from the service organization and the adequacy of the standards under which the service auditor's report was issued.

    b. The auditor should inquire of the management of the user entity about whether the service organization has reported to the not-for-profit entity, or if management is otherwise aware of, any fraud, noncompliance with laws and regulations, or uncorrected misstatements affecting the financial statements.

    c. The auditor should evaluate the design and implementation of the not-for-profit entity's relevant controls that are applied to the transactions processed by the service organization.

    d. All of the above are required audit procedures regarding service organizations.

## TECHNICAL BACKGROUND INFORMATION – PROGRAMMATIC INVESTMENTS

As part of accomplishing their mission, some not-for-profit entities make contributions of programmatic investments instead of cash. **A programmatic investment** is defined as any investment by a not-for-profit entity that meets both of the following criteria:

1. Its primary purpose is to further the tax exempt objectives of the not-for-profit entity.

2. The production of income or the appreciation of the asset is not a significant purpose.

The nature of programmatic investments is to further the mission of the not-for-profit entity, rather than to provide investment income or appreciation of the asset. Accordingly, programmatic investments often have a contribution element. Management should determine whether an investment is programmatic when the initial investment transaction occurs. The contribution element made by the not-for-profit entity should be recorded in accordance with FASB ASC 958-720, *Not-for-Profit Entities – Other Expenses*. For elements other than the contribution element, the programmatic investment should be accounted for consistent with similar non-programmatic investments. For example, receivable elements should be accounted for as receivables, ownership interests should be accounted for in accordance with standards for reporting relationships with related parties, and more.

Common types of programmatic investments are loans, equity interests, or guarantees. Examples include the following:

- Low-interest or interest-free loans to students with demonstrated financial need
- Student loans that will be forgiven upon the completion of a defined amount of community service after graduation
- Loans to small for-profit businesses owned by members of economically disadvantaged groups or individuals who are members of those groups, for whom commercial loans are not available or are not available at affordable interest rates
- Loans, typically of small dollar amounts, made to small businesses or individuals who lack access to banking and related services as a way to help the borrower out of poverty (microfinancing)
- Investments in not-for-profit low income housing projects

- Investments in businesses in deteriorated urban areas under a plan to improve the economy of the area by providing employment or job training for residents
- Investments in not-for-profit entities that have a mission of combating community deterioration
- Guarantees of a not-for-profit entity's debt, which increases the amount of credit available to that not-for-profit because the guarantor assumes part or all of the third-party lender's risk

Loans made to other entities are the most common programmatic investment and can be accounted for using one of two methods. Not-for-profit entities can use an effective interest rate approach or an inherent contribution approach. The not-for-profit entity should determine which method is most appropriate and apply those standards, reporting consistently from period to period. Management should disclose its accounting policy for these programmatic investments. If making programmatic loans is a significant program service, it is recommended that the not-for-profit entity disclose the following additional information:

- The number of loans outstanding
- The average face amount and average carrying amount of the loans at origination and the reason for the difference
- The program purpose that is being accomplished by the loan activity
- The amount of impairment losses in total and by program expense line item(s)

Equity interests that are programmatic investments are typically held in for-profit entities and generally would not have a contribution element. In addition to required disclosures for equity instruments, it is recommended that the not-for-profit entity disclose the following additional information:

- The number of programmatic equity investees
- The carrying amount recognized in the statement of financial position for the programmatic equity investments
- The program purpose that is being accomplished by the programmatic equity relationship
- The amount of impairment losses in total and by program expense line item(s)

Management should consider if the note disclosures about their programmatic investments and explain how those programmatic investments support the program service(s) and mission of the not-for-profit entity.

## Auditing Considerations

There are some unique auditing procedures the auditor may consider for programmatic investments. These procedures include the following:

- Review the accounting policies for programmatic investments.
- Understand the initial investment transaction and determine if it has the characteristics of a programmatic investment.
- Review programmatic investments to determine if an impairment loss should be recognized.
- Inquire whether the not-for-profit entity has guaranteed the debt of other entities. If so, determine the appropriateness of the recorded amount and the appropriateness of the not-for-profit entity's monitoring procedures regarding adjustment of the liability.
- Review disclosures for understandability and completeness.

If the auditor is auditing programmatic investments that include loans, the auditor may review the loan documents to

- determine if the interest rate is appropriate;
- assess the collectibility;

- determine if there is forgiveness of debt; and
- determine if there was a conditional contribution element to the loan. If so, determine if the condition has been met.

If the auditor is auditing programmatic investments that include equity interests, he or she may consider reviewing the investment agreements

- to determine if there are additional rights and privileges that should be recognized. If so, confirm that they have been recorded; and
- to determine whether consolidation is required. If consolidation is not required, determine whether the equity method, cost method, or fair value is required.

## KNOWLEDGE CHECK

2. Which is a requirement for an investment to be considered a programmatic investment?

   a. The investment's primary purpose is to further the tax exempt objectives of the not-for-profit entity, and the asset is not expected to produce income or appreciate in value as a significant purpose.

   b. The investment is not expected to produce income or appreciate in value.

   c. The investment's primary purpose is to further the tax exempt objectives of the not-for-profit entity, and the asset is expected to produce income or appreciate in value.

   d. The investment must have a contribution element.

## TECHNICAL BACKGROUND INFORMATION – GROUP AUDITS

**Group audits** involve an audit of financial statements that include a group of more than one component. The scope of group audits has been greatly expanded under the clarified auditing standards. Auditors should understand that it is not necessary to have another auditor involved in the audit engagement for the audit to be considered a group audit. A group audit is an audit of group financial statements, regardless of how many audit organizations are involved.

Group financial statements include more than consolidated or combined financial statements; they include financial statements of multiple business activities in addition to separate entities, both of which are referred to as components. Components may include subsidiaries, geographical locations, divisions, investments, services, functions, or processes of the not-for-profit entity.

It is possible for an auditor to be both the group auditor and the component auditor. If, historically, an auditor has performed both the group audit and the component audit, the clarified auditing standards include additional requirements the auditor should now consider.

AU-C section 600, *Special Considerations – Audits of Group Financial Statements (Including the Work of Component Auditors)*, addresses the requirements for group audits. An audit of group financial statements includes identifying components of the group and identifying which of those components are significant. The group auditor should have an understanding of all of the significant components, sufficient to assess the risks of material misstatement, whether due to fraud or error, for the group. The group auditor should also have an understanding of the consolidation process, including instructions from group management to the components, sufficient to assess the risks of material misstatement, whether due to error or fraud.

The group engagement partner will either choose to assume responsibility for, and, accordingly, be involved in, the work of any component auditors, or choose not to assume responsibility for the work of any component auditors, and, accordingly, make reference to the audit of the component auditor in the group auditor's report.

Even when the group auditor's report makes reference to the component auditor, there are required communications the group engagement team is to have with the component auditor, and the group engagement team should determine that the materiality thresholds determined by the component auditor are appropriate for purposes of the group audit.

Regardless of whether reference will be made to the component auditor's report, the group engagement team should obtain an understanding of the following:

- Whether a component auditor understands and will comply with the ethical requirements that are relevant to the group audit and, in particular, is independent.
- A component auditor's professional competence.
- The extent, if any, to which the group engagement team will be able to be involved in the work of the component auditor.
- Whether the group engagement team will be able to obtain information affecting the consolidation process from a component auditor.
- Whether a component auditor operates in a regulatory environment that oversees auditors actively.

### Management's Considerations

Group management is responsible for the preparation and fair presentation of the group financial statements. This would include the financial information for each of the components.

Group management not-for-profit is also responsible to design, implement, and maintain controls over financial reporting for the group financial statements.

These group-wide controls should include the consolidation process. If the financial information of a component has been prepared using a different financial reporting framework, different accounting policies, or a different reporting period, than that which is used for the group, management should identify the adjustments necessary to the component's financial information for the fair presentation of the group financial statements in accordance with the applicable financial reporting framework for the group.

## KNOWLEDGE CHECK

3.  Which statement is true regarding group audits?

    a.  A group audit is an audit in which an auditor refers to another auditor's report.
    b.  Group audits always involve more than one audit organization.
    c.  Regardless of whether reference will be made to the component auditor's report, the group engagement team should obtain an understanding about whether the group engagement team will be able to obtain information affecting the consolidation process from a component auditor.
    d.  If the group auditor's report refers to a component auditor, the group auditor's responsibility consists solely of obtaining the component auditor's report.

# EXEMPT ORGANIZATIONS GLOSSARY

## GOVERNMENTAL TERMINOLOGY

**Accounting System** – The methods and records established to identify, assemble, analyze, classify, record, and report a government's transactions and to maintain accountability for the related assets and liabilities.

**Accrual Basis of Accounting** – The recording of financial effects on a government of transactions and other events and circumstances that have consequences for the government in the periods in which those transactions, events, and circumstances occur, rather than only in the periods in which cash is received or paid by the government.

**Ad Valorem Tax** – A tax based on value (such as a property tax).

**Advance From Other Funds** – An asset account used to record noncurrent portions of a long-term debt owed by one fund to another fund within the same reporting entity. (See **Due to Other Funds** and *Interfund Receivable/Payable*).

**Agency Funds** – A fund normally used to account for assets held by a government as an agent for individuals, private organizations or other governments and/ or other funds.

**Appropriation** – A legal authorization granted by a legislative body to make expenditures and to incur obligations for specific purposes. An appropriation is usually limited in amount and time it may be expended.

**Assigned Fund Balance** – A portion of fund balance that includes amounts that are constrained by the government's intent to be used for specific purposes, but that are neither restricted nor committed.

**Basis of Accounting** – A term used to refer to *when* revenues, expenditures, expenses, and transfers, and related assets and liabilities are recognized in the accounts and reported in the financial statements. Specifically, it relates to the timing of the measurements made, regardless of the nature of the measurement. (See **Accrual Basis of Accounting, Cash Basis of Accounting,** and **Modified Accrual Basis of Accounting**).

**Bond** – A written promise to pay a specified sum of money (the face value or principal amount) at a specified date or dates in the future (the maturity dates[s]), together with periodic interest at a specified rate. Sometimes, however, all or a substantial part of the interest is included in the face value of the security. The difference between a note and bond is that the latter is issued for a longer period and requires greater legal formality.

**Business Type Activities** – Those activities of a government carried out primarily to provide specific services in exchange for a specific user charge.

**Capital Grants** – Grants restricted by the grantor for the acquisition and/ or construction of (a) capital asset(s).

**Capital Projects Fund** – A fund used to account for and report financial resources that are restricted, committed, or assigned to expenditures for capital outlays, including the acquisition or construction of capital facilities and other capital assets. Capital project funds exclude those types of capital-related outflows financed by proprietary funds or for assets that will be held in trust for individuals, private organizations, or other governments.

**Cash Basis of Accounting** – A basis of accounting that requires the recognition of transactions only when cash is received or disbursed.

**Committed Fund Balance** – A portion of fund balance that includes amounts that can only be used for specific purposes pursuant to constraints imposed by formal action of the government's highest level of decision-making authority.

**Consumption Method** – The method of accounting that requires the recognition of an expenditure/ expense as inventories are used.

**Contributed Capital** – Contributed capital is created when a general capital asset is *transferred* to a proprietary fund or when a grant is received that is externally restricted to capital acquisition or construction. Contributions restricted to capital acquisition and construction and capital assets received from developers are reported in the operating statement as a separate item after nonoperating revenues and expenses.

**Debt Service Fund** – A fund used to account for and report financial resources that are restricted, committed, or assigned to expenditure for principal and interest. Debt service funds should be used to report resources if legally mandated. Financial resources that are being accumulated for principal and interest maturing in future years should also be reported debt service funds.

**Deferred Revenue** – Amounts for which asset recognition criteria (receivable) have been met, but for which revenue recognition criteria have not been. Under the modified accrual basis of accounting, amounts that are measurable but not available are classified as deferred revenue. Cash received in advance of the period of applicability is also recorded as deferred revenue.

**Deficit** – (a) The excess of the liabilities of a fund over its assets. (b) The excess of expenditures over revenues during an accounting period, or in the case of proprietary funds, the excess of expenses over revenues during an accounting period.

**Disbursement** – A payment made in cash or by check. Expenses are only recognized at the time physical cash is disbursed.

**Due From Other Funds** – A current asset account used to indicate account reflecting amounts owed to a particular fund by another fund for goods sold or services rendered. This account includes only short-term obligations on open account, not interfund loans.

**Due to Other Funds** – A current liability account reflecting amounts owed by a particular fund to another fund for goods sold or services rendered. This account includes only short-term obligations on an open account, not interfund loans.

**Fund Financial Statements** – Each fund has its own set of self-balancing accounts and fund financial statements that focus on information about the government's governmental, proprietary, and fiduciary fund types.

**Enabling Legislation** – Legislation that authorizes a government to assess, levy, charge, or otherwise mandate payment of resources from external resource providers, and includes a legally enforceable requirement that those resources be used for the specific purposes stipulated in the legislation.

**Encumbrances** – Commitments related to unperformed (executory) contracts for goods or services. Used in budgeting, encumbrances are *not* GAAP expenditures or liabilities, but represent the estimated amount of expenditures ultimately to result if unperformed contracts in process are completed.

**Enterprise Fund** – A fund established to account for operations financed and operated in a manner similar to private business enterprises (such as gas, utilities, transit systems, and parking garages). Usually, the governing body intends that costs of providing goods or services to the general public be recovered primarily through user charges.

**Expenditures** – Decreases in net financial resources. Expenditures include current operating expenses requiring the present or future use of net current assets, debt service and capital outlays, intergovernmental grants, entitlements, and shared revenues.

**Expenses** – Outflows or other using up of assets or incurrences of liabilities, or a combination of both, from delivering or producing goods, rendering services, or carrying out other activities that constitute the entity's ongoing major or central operations.

**Fund** – A fiscal and accounting entity with a self-balancing set of accounts in which cash and other financial resources, all related liabilities and residual equities, or balances, and changes therein, are recorded and segregated to carry on specific activities or attain certain objectives in accordance with special regulations, restrictions, or limitations.

**Fund Balance** – The difference between fund assets and fund liabilities of the generic fund types within the governmental category of funds.

**Fund Type** – The 11 generic funds that all transactions of a government are recorded into. The 11 fund types are as follows: general, special revenue, debt service, capital projects, permanent, enterprise, internal service, private purpose trust, pension trust, investment trust, and agency.

**GASB** – The Governmental Accounting Standards Board (GASB) was organized in 1984 by the Financial Accounting Foundation (FAF) to establish standards of financial accounting and reporting for state and local governmental entities. Its standards guide the preparation of external financial reports of those entities.

**General Fund** – The fund within the governmental category used to account for all financial resources except those required to be accounted for in another governmental fund.

**General-Purpose Governments** – General-purpose governments are governmental entities that provide a range of services, such as states, cities, counties, towns, and villages.

**Governmental Funds** – Funds used to account for the acquisition, use, and balances of spendable financial resources and the related current liabilities, except those accounted for in proprietary funds and fiduciary funds. Essentially, these funds are accounting segregations of financial resources. Spendable assets are assigned to a particular government fund type according to the purposes for which they may or must be used. Current liabilities are assigned to the fund type from which they are to be paid. The difference between the assets and liabilities of governmental fund types is referred to as fund balance. The measurement focus in these funds types is on the determination of financial position and changes in financial position (sources, uses, and balances of financial resources) rather than on net income determination.

**Government-Wide Financial Statements** – The government-wide financial statements are highly aggregated financial statements that present financial information for all assets (including infrastructure capital assets), liabilities, and net assets of a primary government and its component units, except for fiduciary funds. The government-wide financial statements use the economic resources measurement focus and accrual basis of accounting.

**Infrastructure Assets** – Infrastructure assets are long-lived capital assets that normally are stationary in nature and normally can be preserved for a significantly greater number of years than most capital assets. Examples of infrastructure assets are roads, bridges, tunnels, drainage systems, water and sewer systems, dams, and lighting systems. Buildings, except those that are an ancillary part of a network of infrastructure assets, are not considered infrastructure assets.

**Internal Service Fund** – A generic fund type within the proprietary category used to account for the financing of goods or services provided by one department or agency to other departments or agencies of a government, or to other governments, on a cost-reimbursement basis.

**Investment Trust Fund** – A generic fund type within the fiduciary category used by a government in a fiduciary capacity, such as to maintain its cash and investment pool for other governments.

**Major Funds** – A government's general fund (or its equivalent), other individual governmental type, and enterprise funds that meet specific quantitative criteria, and any other governmental or enterprise fund that a government's officials believe is particularly important to financial statement users.

**Management's Discussion and Analysis (MD&A)** – MD&A is RSI that introduces the basic financial statements by presenting certain financial information as well as management's analytical insights on that information.

**Measurement Focus** – The accounting convention that determines (a) which assets and which liabilities are included on a government's balance sheet and where they are reported, and (b) whether an operating statement presents information on the flow of financial resources (revenues and expenditures) or information on the flow of economic resources (revenues and expenses).

**Modified Accrual Basis of Accounting** – The basis of accounting adapted to the governmental fund type measurement focus. Revenues and other financial resource increments are recognized when they become both *measurable* and *available to finance expenditures of the current period. Available* means collectible in the current period or soon enough thereafter to be used to pay liabilities of the current period. Expenditures are recognized when the fund liability is incurred and expected to be paid from current resources except for (a) inventories of materials and supplies that may be considered expenditures either when purchased or when used, and (b) prepaid insurance and similar items that may be considered expenditures either when paid for or when consumed. All governmental funds are accounted for using the modified accrual basis of accounting in fund financial statements.

**Modified Approach** – Rules that allow infrastructure assets that are part of a network or subsystem of a network not to be depreciated as long as certain requirements are met.

**Nonspendable Fund Balance** – The portion of fund valance that includes amounts that cannot be spent because they are either (a) not in spendable form, or (b) legally or contractually required to be maintained intact.

**Pension Trust Fund** – A trust fund used to account for a PERS. Pension trust funds use the accrual basis of accounting and the flow of economic resources measurement focus.

Permanent Fund – A generic fund type under the governmental category used to report resources that are legally restricted to the extent that only earnings, and not principal, may be used for purposes that support the reporting government's programs and, therefore, are for the benefit of the government or its citizenry. (Permanent funds do not include private-purpose trust funds, which should be used when the government is required to use the principal or earnings for the benefit of individuals, private organizations, or other governments).

Private Purpose Trust Fund – A general fund type under the fiduciary category used to report resources held and administered by the reporting government acting in a fiduciary capacity for individuals, other governments, or private organizations.

Proprietary Funds – The government category used to account for a government's ongoing organizations and activities that are similar to those often found in the private sector (these are enterprise and internal service funds). All assets, liabilities, equities, revenues, expenses, and transfers relating to the government's business and quasi-business activities are accounted for through proprietary funds. Proprietary funds should apply all applicable GASB pronouncements and those GAAP applicable to similar businesses in the private sector, unless those conflict with GASB pronouncements. These funds use the accrual basis of accounting in conjunction with the flow of economic resources measurement focus.

Purchases Method – The method under which inventories are recorded as expenditures when acquired.

Restricted Fund Balance – Portion of fund valance that reflects constraints placed on the use of resources (other than nonspendable items) that are either (a) externally imposed by creditor such as through debt covenants, grantors, contributors, or laws or regulations of other governments, or (b) imposed by law through constitutional provisions or enabling legislation.

Required Supplementary Information (RSI) – GAAP specify that certain information be presented as RSI.

Special-Purpose Governments – Special-purpose governments are legally separate entities that perform only one activity or only a few activities, such as cemetery districts, school districts, colleges and universities, utilities, hospitals and other health care organizations, and public employee retirement systems.

Special Revenue Fund – A fund that *must* have revenue or proceeds from specific revenue sources which are either restricted or committed for a specific purpose other than debt service or capital projects. This definition means that in order to be considered a special revenue fund, there must be one or more revenue sources upon which reporting the activity in a separate fund is predicated.

Transfers – All interfund transfers, such as legally authorized transfers from a fund receiving revenue to a fund through which the resources are to be expended, where there is no intent to repay. Interfund transfers are recorded on the operating statement.

Unassigned Fund Balance – Residual classification for the general fund. This classification represents fund balance that has not been assigned to other funds and that has not been restricted, committed, or assigned to specific purposes within the general fund. The general fund should be the only fund that reports a positive unassigned fund valance amount. In other funds, if expenditures incurred for specific purposes exceeded the amounts restricted, committed, or assigned to those purposes,

Unrestricted Fund Balance – The total of committed fund balance, assigned fund balance, and unassigned fund balance.

# NOT-FOR-PROFIT TERMINOLOGY

**Charitable Lead Trust** – A trust established in connection with a split-interest agreement, in which the not-for-profit organization receives distributions during the agreement's term. Upon termination of the trust, the remainder of the trust assets is paid to the donor or to third-party beneficiaries designated by the donor.

**Charitable Remainder Trust** – A trust established in connection with a split-interest agreement, in which the donor or a third-party beneficiary receives specified distributions during the agreement's term. Upon termination of the trust, a not-for-profit organization receives the assets remaining in the trust.

**Collections** – Works of art, historical treasures, or similar assets that are (a) held for public exhibition, education, or research in furtherance of public service rather than financial gain, (b) protected, kept unencumbered, cared for, and preserved, and (c) subject to an organizational policy that requires the proceeds of items that are sold to be used to acquire other items for collections.

**Conditional Promise to Give** – A promise to give that depends on the occurrence of a specified future and uncertain event to bind the promisor.

**Contribution** – An unconditional transfer of cash or other assets to an entity or a settlement or cancellation of its liabilities in a voluntary nonreciprocal transfer by another entity acting other than as an owner.

**Costs of Joint Activities** – Costs of joint activities are costs incurred for a joint activity. Costs of joint activities may include joint costs and costs other than joint costs. Costs other than joint costs are costs that are identifiable with a particular function, such as program, fundraising, management and general, and membership development costs.

**Donor-Imposed Restriction** – A donor stipulation that specifies a use for the contributed asset that is more specific than broad limits resulting from the nature of the organization, the environment in which it operates, and the purposes specified in its articles of incorporation or bylaws, or comparable documents for an unincorporated association. A restriction on an organization's use of the asset contributed may be temporary or permanent.

**Functional Classification** – A method of grouping expenses according to the purpose for which the costs are incurred. The primary functional classifications are program services and supporting activities.

**Joint Activity** – A joint activity is an activity that is part of the fundraising function and has elements of one or more other functions, such as programs, management and general, membership development, or any other functional category used by the entity.

**Joint Costs** – Joint costs are the costs of conducting joint activities that are not identifiable with a particular component of the activity.

**Natural Expense Classification** – A method of grouping expenses according to the kinds of economic benefits received in incurring those expenses. Examples of natural expense classifications include salaries and wages, employee benefits, supplies, rent, and utilities.

**Permanently Restricted Net Assets** – The part of the net assets of a not-for-profit organization resulting (a) from contributions and other inflows of assets whose use by the organization is limited by donor-imposed stipulations that neither expire by passage of time nor can be fulfilled or otherwise removed by actions of the organization, (b) from other asset enhancements and diminishments subject to the same kinds of stipulations, and (c) from reclassifications from (or to) other classes of net assets as a consequence of donor-imposed stipulations.

**Promise to Give** – A written or oral agreement to contribute cash or other assets to another entity. A promise to give may be either conditional or unconditional.

**Temporarily Restricted Net Assets** – The part of the net assets of a not-for-profit organization resulting (a) from contributions and other inflows of assets whose use by the organization is limited by donor-imposed stipulations that either expire by the passage of time or can be fulfilled and removed by actions of the organization pursuant to those stipulations, (b) from other asset enhancements and diminishments subject to the same kinds of stipulations, and (c) from reclassifications to (or from) other classes of net assets as a consequence of donor-imposed stipulations, their expiration by passage of time, or their fulfillment and removal by actions of the organization pursuant to those stipulations.

**Unrestricted Net Assets** – The part of net assets of a not-for-profit organization that is neither permanently restricted nor temporarily restricted by donor-imposed stipulations.

# SINGLE AUDIT &YELLOW BOOK TERMINOLOGY

**Attestation Engagements** – Attestation engagements concern examining, reviewing, or performing agreed-upon procedures on a subject matter or an assertion about a subject matter and reporting on the results.

**Compliance Supplement** – A document issued annually in the Spring by the OMB to provide guidance to auditors.

**Data Collection Form** – A form submitted to the Federal Audit Clearinghouse which provides information about the auditor, the auditee and its federal programs, and the results of the audit.

**Federal Financial Assistance** – Assistance that non-federal entities receive or administer in the form of grants, loans, loan guarantees, property, cooperative agreements, interest subsidies, insurance, food commodities, direct appropriations, or other assistance, but does not include amounts received as reimbursement for services rendered to individuals in accordance with guidance issued by the Director.

**Financial Audits** – Financial audits are primarily concerned with providing reasonable assurance about whether financial statements are presented fairly, in all material respects, in conformity with generally accepted accounting principles (GAAP) or with a comprehensive basis of accounting other than GAAP.

**GAGAS** – Generally Accepted Government Auditing Standards issued by the GAO. They are also commonly known as the Yellow Book.

**GAO** – The United States Government Accountability Office. Among their responsibilities is the issuance of Generally Accepted Government Auditing Standards (a.k.a. the Yellow Book).

**OMB** – The Office of Management and Budget. OMB assists the President in the development and implementation of budget, program, management, and regulatory policies.

**Pass-Through Entity** – A non-federal entity that provides federal awards to a subrecipient to carry out a federal program.

**Performance Audits** – Performance audits entail an objective and systematic examination of evidence to provide an independent assessment of the performance and management of a program against objective criteria as well as assessments that provide a prospective focus or that synthesize information on best practices or cross-cutting issues.

**Program-Specific Audit** – An audit of one federal program.

**Single Audit** – An audit of a non-federal entity that includes the entity's financial statements and Federal awards.

**Single Audit Guide** – This AICPA Audit Guide formally titled Government Auditing Standards and Circular A-133 Audits (the Single Audit Guide) is the former Statement of Position (SOP) 98-3. The Single Audit Guide provides guidance on the auditor's responsibilities when conducting a single audit or program-specific audit in accordance with the Single Audit Act and Circular A-133.

**Subrecipient** – A non-federal entity that receives federal awards through another non-federal entity to carry out a federal program, but does not include an individual who receives financial assistance through such awards.

# INDEX

# CASE STUDIES IN NOT-FOR-PROFIT ACCOUNTING AND AUDITING

By Bruce Chase, Ph.D., CPA; Laura Lindal, CPA;
William Wagner, CPA

## Solutions

The AICPA offers a free, daily, e-mailed newsletter covering the day's top business and financial articles as well as video content, research and analysis concerning CPAs and those who work with the accounting profession. Visit the CPA Letter Daily news box on the www.aicpa.org home page to sign up. You can opt out at any time, and only the AICPA can use your e-mail address or personal information.

Have a technical accounting or auditing question? So did 23,000 other professionals who contacted the AICPA's accounting and auditing Technical Hotline last year. The objectives of the hotline are to enhance members' knowledge and application of professional judgment by providing free, prompt, high-quality technical assistance by phone concerning issues related to: accounting principles and financial reporting; auditing, attestation, compilation and review standards. The team extends this technical assistance to representatives of governmental units. The hotline can be reached at 1-877-242-7212.

# SOLUTIONS

## CHAPTER 1

Case Study Solutions

There are several deficiencies in the statement prepared by Tom, including the following:

- The statement does not report a change in total net assets for the year.
- The statement reports the using up of restricted resources as expenses in temporarily restricted net assets. All expenses should be recorded as decreases in unrestricted net assets. Using resources to meet a temporary donor-stipulated restriction would decrease temporarily restricted net assets and increase unrestricted net assets simultaneously.
- It appears that all gifts were recorded as increases in unrestricted net assets, and the restricted gifts then transferred to the proper class of net assets. Restricted gifts should be recorded directly in the proper class of net assets.
- The statement uses the term expenditures instead of expenses. The statement should report expenses, not expenditures.
- The statement reports depreciation. This is not a functional classification of expense.

The following are additional observations about Tom's statement. They are not errors.

- The statement is titled "statement of operations," not the statement of activities. It is acceptable to label this statement something other than the statement of activities.
- The statement reports a "loss from operations." This is acceptable. An organization may choose to report some intermediate measure of operations, such as operating revenues over expenses.
- The statement does not report total revenue or expenses. Revenues, gains, expenses, losses, and reclassifications can be arranged in a variety of orders. There is no requirement to report totals for these items.

Solutions to Knowledge Check Questions

1.
   a. Correct. Voluntary health and welfare organizations are required to present a statement of functional expenses.
   b. Incorrect. Not-for-profit entities present financial statements showing aggregate information about the entity.
   c. Incorrect. The general purpose financial statements include the accompanying notes to the financial statements.
   d. Incorrect. The general-purpose financial statements for not-for-profit organizations are different from businesses.

**2.**

    a.   Correct. Information about the nature and amounts of different types of permanent restrictions or temporary restrictions on net assets should either be reported on the face of the statement or in the notes to the financial statement.

    b.   Incorrect. Unrestricted net assets can use separate lines to report self-imposed limits (designations) on net assets.

    c.   Incorrect. Assets and liabilities can be presented in a number of ways to provide information about liquidity.

    d.   Incorrect. Totals are required for assets, liabilities, and net assets.

**3.**

    a.   Incorrect. The amount of change in permanently restricted net assets must be reported.

    b.   Incorrect. The amount of change in temporarily restricted net assets must be reported.

    c.   Correct. The amount of change in unrestricted net assets must be reported.

    d.   Incorrect. The amount of change in net assets must be reported.

**4.**

    a.   Correct. Events that increase one class of net assets and decrease another class of net assets (reclassifications) simultaneously are reported as separate items in the statement of activities.

    b.   Incorrect. Revenues, gains, expenses, losses, and reclassifications can be arranged in a variety of orders.

    c.   Incorrect. Revenues are reported as increases in unrestricted net assets unless the use of assets received is limited by donor-imposed restrictions

    d.   Incorrect. Expenses can be displayed either by natural or functional classifications in the statement of activities.

**5.**

    a.   Incorrect. Cash flow from operating activities would include, if applicable, agency transactions.

    b.   Correct. Because cash restricted for long-term purposes is normally excluded from cash available for current use, a cash contribution for a long-term purpose would normally be reported as both a cash inflow from financing activities and a cash outflow from investing activities.

    c.   Incorrect. Organizations may present the statement of cash flows using either the direct or indirect method.

    d.   Incorrect. Using the direct method, NFP must reconcile cash flow activities to change in net assets.

**6.**

    a.   Incorrect. Voluntary health and welfare organizations are required to report a statement of functional expenses.

    b.   Correct. Voluntary health and welfare organizations depend primarily on contributions from the general public.

    c.   Incorrect. The statement of functional expenses provides additional information on how resources are used.

    d.   Incorrect. The statement of functional expenses does provide information on functional and natural classification of expenses.

**7.**

   a. Correct. Organizations may report columns in the financial statements to convey a variety of information.
   b. Incorrect. Some organizations find it useful to break out operating activities from other activities.
   c. Incorrect. For some organizations, fund information remains important for external financial reporting.
   d. Incorrect. There is flexibility in the number of columns in the statement of activities.

# CHAPTER 2

Case Study Solutions

| Item | Net Asset Classification | Reason |
|------|--------------------------|--------|
| The $500,000 of student fees set aside for a future student center | unrestricted net assets | Only a donor can impose a stipulation that makes an amount either temporarily or permanently restricted. This amount is from student fees. Any limitation on the use of assets should be disclosed. This amount can also be reported as a designated amount of unrestricted net assets. |
| The $2,500,000 collected and spent on the new science building | temporarily restricted net assets | The college has adopted a policy that implies a time restriction on the use of cash restricted to the purchase of long-lived assets that expires over the assets' expected useful lives. Because the building will not be put into service until next year, the full amount would be reported as temporarily restricted. |
| The $100,000 located in the debt reserve fund | unrestricted net assets | Only a donor can impose a stipulation that makes an amount either temporarily or permanently restricted. The college has a contractual obligation to set this amount aside and would need to disclose this requirement. |
| The $75,000 of outstanding pledges | temporarily restricted net assets | The pledges are to support the general operations; however, unconditional promises to give with payments due in future periods should be reported as temporarily restricted contributions unless the donor expressly stipulates, or circumstances surrounding the receipt of the promise make clear, that the donor intended it to be used to support activities of the current period. |

| Item | Net Asset Classification | Reason |
|------|--------------------------|--------|
| The $500,000 received from the bequest | unrestricted net assets | Donor stipulations should not be considered restrictions unless the use of the assets is more specific than the broad limits imposed by the organization's purpose and nature. The bequest was to be used for educational purposes, and the main purpose of the college is education. In addition, only a donor can make a contribution permanently restricted, not the board of trustees. This amount can also be reported as a designated amount of unrestricted net assets. |
| The $10,000 senior gift | unrestricted net assets | Although the amount is for a restricted purpose, the college has adopted a policy that reports contributions with donor-imposed restrictions that are met in the same period that the contribution is received as unrestricted support. The college spent more than $10,000 on books. |

Solutions to Knowledge Check Questions

**1.**

a. Incorrect. All net assets not classified as permanently or temporarily restricted are unrestricted.
b. Incorrect. Donor-imposed stipulations can result in temporarily restricted net assets.
c. Correct. Donor-imposed stipulations can result in permanently restricted net assets.
d. Incorrect. Contributions without donor-imposed stipulations are classified as unrestricted.

**2.**

a. Correct. Some organizations receive contributions of long-lived assets or cash and other assets restricted to the purchase of long-lived assets.
b. Incorrect. Often, the donor will not expressly stipulate how or how long the long-lived asset must be used by the organization.
c. Incorrect. An organization may adopt one of two policies related to contributions of long-lived assets. The organization may either imply a time restriction on the use of such assets that expires over the asset's expected useful lives or the organization may adopt a policy of implying no time restriction. Where a time restriction is implied, contributions of long-lived assets may be reported as temporarily restricted, and the restriction would be met over the asset's expected life. Where no implied time restriction exists, contributions of long-lived assets are unrestricted.
d. Incorrect. An organization may adopt one of two policies related to contributions of long-lived assets.

**3.**

a. Incorrect. In some cases, donor-imposed restrictions are met in the same period that the contribution is received.
b. Correct. Temporary restrictions limit the use of assets by donor-imposed stipulations that either expire by passage of time or can be fulfilled and removed by actions of the organization pursuant to those stipulations.
c. Incorrect. Restrictions may be stipulated explicitly by the donor in a written or oral communication accompanying the gift.
d. Incorrect. Organization have a policy choice on how to report contribution with donor-imposed restriction that are met in the same period as either unrestricted or temporarily restricted.

# CHAPTER 3

Case Study Solutions

1. The identification of fraud risk factors will vary by person and his or her understanding of the organization, its internal control, and its processes. A few fraud risk factors could be the following:

- The office manager's hours were cut to part time. The office manager may have financial difficulties due to this decrease in pay, providing increased incentive and rationalization to commit fraud.
- The resource development manager (RDM) may have recognized that the position was in jeopardy, providing increased incentive and rationalization to commit fraud.
- The decrease in ticket sales and donations at the annual dinner is understandable in the current economy. However, it could also be due to skimming receipts.
- Time sheets could be completed for hours not worked.
- Unauthorized disbursements for small amounts or similar amounts to authorized disbursements could be made by the office manager on unsigned or forged checks and not be detected, or detected in a timely manner.
- The office manager could divert cash donations from the annual dinner and not be detected, or detected in a timely manner.
- Allocation of employees' time for functional purposes could be an indication of fraudulent financial reporting.
- Lack of monitoring or oversight of the functions performed by the office manager.
- There may be temporarily restricted net assets due to provisions in the grant agreements or restrictions that were implied to attendees at the dinner and silent auction.

2. The identification of procedures to be performed to address risks of fraud in revenue recognition will vary by audit team and should be designed to address the assessed risks of material misstatement due to fraud. Items to consider may include the following:

- Contribution revenue from the dinner and silent auction appears to be straightforward in that it is recorded when received.
- There may be non-recognition of contribution revenue, due to diverted receipts.
- Contributions from grants may involve recognition in periods of more than one fiscal year, depending on the timing of the grant.
- Contributions may also involve purpose or time restrictions that have not been recognized in the accounting records.
- Confirmation with granting agencies regarding the purpose, amount, and timing of the grant funds.
- Inquiry of donors who attended the dinner regarding their understanding of the purpose of the donation.
- Review of deposit tickets for the deposit of currency or coin to indicate completeness of revenue recognition.
- Comparison of list of items auctioned to thank-you letters prepared by the RDM and to the bid sheets, noting that there was a bid sheet for each item received.
- Review of schedule of tickets sold reconciled to funds received (prepared by the RDM) and reconciled to revenue recorded in the general ledger.

- Comparison of number of dinner tickets sold in the current year to number of dinner tickets sold in the prior year, and comparison of that information to total revenue from dinner for both years.
- Comparison of the amount and types of items donated for the auction in the current year to the amount and types of items donated for the auction in the prior year.

3. The audit team will need to exercise professional skepticism even though the firm has a good working relationship with the client. Procedures performed to address the fraud risk of management override of controls by client depend on its internal control and its processes.

   The audit team may perform the following procedures:

   - Examination of journal entries and other adjustments for evidence of material misstatement due to fraud.
   - Review of functional allocation of expenses for biases that could result in a material misstatement due to fraud.
   - Inquiry of personnel or board members regarding incentives to misstate functional allocation of expenses.
   - Evaluation of business rationale for significant, unusual transactions.
   - Inquiry of personnel or board members regarding the existence of grant restrictions or requirements.
   - Inquiry of personnel, other than the executive director, regarding how a misstatement due to fraud could occur, if they know of any allegations that a misstatement due to fraud did occur, if they believe a misstatement due to fraud did occur.

   Inquiry of personnel regarding personal situations of other employees that could be causing financial hardship or situations of other employees where they appear to be living beyond the means provided by their employment with Struggling NFP.

Solutions to Knowledge Check Questions

**1.**
   a. Correct. Not-for-profits may experience incentives or pressures to increase the percentage of program services compared to total expenses.
   b. Incorrect. It is unlikely that not-for-profits would experience incentives or pressures to increase the percentage of fundraising services compared to total expenses.
   c. Incorrect. Not-for-profits may experience incentives or pressures to report restricted gifts as unrestricted.
   d. Incorrect. Not-for-profits may experience pressure to recognize revenues belonging to future periods, not expenses.

**2.**
   a. Incorrect. Not-for-profits may experience incentives or pressures to inappropriately allocate costs to grants.
   b. Correct. Not-for-profits typically do not experience incentives or pressures to report results similar to for-profit entities.
   c. Incorrect. Not-for-profits may experience incentives or pressures to recognize revenue belonging to future periods so as not to show a negative change in net assets.
   d. Incorrect. Not-for-profits may experience incentives or pressures for misclassifications that have tax consequences or affect an organization's exempt status.

**3.**

    a.  Incorrect. Inquiries regarding knowledge of fraud can provide valuable information regarding fraud risk factors.

    b.  Correct. Inquiries regarding experience with fraud would be the least likely types of inquiries to provide valuable information regarding fraud risk factors.

    c.  Incorrect. Inquiries regarding allegations of fraud can provide valuable information regarding fraud risk factors.

    d.  Incorrect. Inquiries regarding potential ways fraud could occur can provide valuable information regarding fraud risk factors.

**4.**

    a.  Incorrect. Analytical procedures that merely compare current results to prior period results will not usually identify an ongoing fraud.

    b.  Incorrect. Depending on the analytical procedures performed, the procedures may not provide valuable information regarding fraud risk factors.

    c.  Incorrect. The auditor should use a combination of procedures to address the risk of material misstatement due to fraud, including inquiries, analytical procedures, and other information that may be helpful to identify fraud risks.

    d.  Correct. Discussion of fraud risk factors among the audit team should always involve the key members of the audit team.

**5.**

    a.  Incorrect. An audit team's overall response on how the audit is conducted includes the consideration of the assignment of personnel and supervision.

    b.  Correct. An audit team's overall response on how the audit is conducted should include the consideration of accounting principles selected and applied by the client.

    c.  Incorrect. An audit team's overall response on how the audit is conducted includes the skills, knowledge, and experience of the personnel assigned to the audit team rather than the number of personnel assigned to the engagement team.

    d.  Incorrect. An audit team's overall response on how the audit is conducted should include the use of unpredictability when designing the nature, timing, and extent of auditing procedures.

**6.**

    a.  Incorrect. Improper revenue recognition includes improper classification of revenue among the three net asset classes.

    b.  Incorrect. Improper revenue recognition does not consider the classification of related expenses.

    c.  Correct. Improper revenue recognition includes recognizing conditional promises to give as unconditional.

    d.  Incorrect. Improper revenue recognition includes recognizing intentions to give as promises to give.

| Situation | Is the promise to give conditional or unconditional? | When would you record the promise to give? |
|---|---|---|
| The executive director of college A approaches Sam Jones and discusses the potential construction of a new Athletic Building on the campus. The projected costs are $10,000,000 per the architect's plans and estimates. Sam Jones is an alumnus of the college and was an All American hockey player who also played professional hockey. The building will include a hockey arena, basketball complex, and other indoor sports. Sam Jones indicates he will commit $500,000 provided the building campaign raises the necessary funds to complete construction. | The commitment is a conditional promise to give. It is conditioned on the college raising another $9,500,000 in order to cover the construction costs of the building. | The promise would be recognized when all funds were committed. |
| The executive director of college A approaches the Wagner Foundation which was formed by a former graduate who retired as a partner from a Big 4 CPA firm. This foundation makes grants to local charities from their investment earnings each year. He indicates "If the Foundation will commit $500,000 to the campaign, we will place the former graduate's name on the cornerstone of the building as a Platinum Contributor." The Foundation sends the college a commitment letter for the $500,000, "provided the college does place Mr. Wagner's name on the cornerstone of the building as a Platinum Contributor." | This is an unconditional promise to give. Even though the Foundation indicated "provided the college does place Mr. Wagner's name on the cornerstone of the building as a Platinum Contributor", it is within the college's ability to have that occur with no interference by another contributor. | The promise would be recognized when the Foundation's commitment letter arrived at the college. |
| The executive director of college A now approaches another graduate who has substantial business interests. Mr. Smith has contributed to the college in the past. He tells Mr. Smith that he has raised approximately $3,000,000 of the $10,000,000 needed to construct the building. Mr. Smith indicates he needs to think about it.<br>A week later, Mr. Smith sends a letter to college A indicating that he could commit $100,000 a year for the next five years "provided you name the facility the H.G. Smith Athletic Building." | This is a conditional promise to give. It is conditioned on the college naming the building "H.G. Smith Athletic Building." | The promise would be recognized if, and when, the board of directors agrees to have the facility named for Mr. Smith. |

| Situation | Is the promise to give conditional or unconditional? | When would you record the promise to give? |
|---|---|---|
| Later in the campaign, the executive director of college A now has commitments totaling $8,000,000 from various entities. He approaches Widget Makers, Inc., a large international company in the area that is privately owned by two families. All the family members have attended and graduated from college A. As he talks to the CEO and President of the Board, Mr. Gotcha and Mr. Now, they indicate that they would be willing to commit the remaining $2,000,000 provided the college names the facility the "Widget Makers Athletic Complex." The executive director indicates that he has a commitment of $500,000 from another graduate that wants the building named after him. Mr. Gotcha and Mr. Now both laugh and say simultaneously "We will then commit $2,500,000!" | This is a conditional promise to give. This condition is in the hands of the board of directors of the college. | The promise would be recognized if, and when, the board of directors agrees to have the facility named "Widget Makers Athletic Complex." (**Note:** This situation makes the conditional promise from Mr. Smith null and void.) |

Solutions to Knowledge Check Questions

1.

a. Correct. When discussing promises to give, a vital distinction is whether the promise to give is unconditional or conditional.
b. Incorrect. A promise to give may be either conditional or unconditional.
c. Incorrect. An unconditional promise to give shall be recognized when it is received.
d. Incorrect. An unconditional promise to give is recognized as revenue when the cash or asset is received.

2.

a. Correct. Not-for-profits may enter into written agreements with donors involving future nonreciprocal transfers of cash.
b. Incorrect. Not-for-profits may enter into written agreements with donors involving future nonreciprocal transfers of assets.
c. Incorrect. Not-for-profits may enter into written agreements with donors involving future nonreciprocal transfers of services.
d. Incorrect. Not-for-profits may not enter into written agreements with donors when the written agreements are revocable involving future transfer of assets.

**3.**

    a.   Incorrect. Not-for-profits may enter into oral agreements with donors involving future nonreciprocal transfers of cash.

    b.   Incorrect. Not-for-profits may enter into oral agreements with donors involving future nonreciprocal transfers of assets.

    c.   Correct. Not-for-profits may enter into oral agreements with donors involving future nonreciprocal transfers of services.

    d.   Incorrect. Not-for-profits may not enter into oral agreements with donors when the oral agreements are revocable involving future transfer of assets.

**4.**

    a.   Correct. Not-for-profits may receive communications that are intentions to give, rather than promises to give.

    b.   Incorrect. Solicitations for donations that clearly include wording such as "information to be used for budget purposes only" are intentions to give rather than promises to give and should not be reported as contributions.

    c.   Incorrect. Solicitations for donations that clearly and explicitly allow resource providers to rescind their indications that they will give are intentions to give rather than promises to give and should not be reported as contributions.

    d.   Incorrect. Intentions to give are always recorded when the intention is given to the not-for-profits.

**5.**

    a.   Correct. Promises to give that are silent about payment terms but otherwise are clearly unconditional shall be accounted for as unconditional promises to give.

    b.   Incorrect. Some donor stipulations do not clearly state whether the right to receive payment or the delivery of promised assets depends on meeting those stipulations.

    c.   Incorrect. The absence of a specified time for transfer of cash or other assets, by itself, does not necessarily lead to a conclusion that a promise to give is ambiguous.

    d.   Incorrect. Promises to give are like intentions to give and should not be recognized until the cash or asset is received.

# CHAPTER 5

Case Study Solutions

1.   Based on the information provided, it appears that the grant from the local foundation is a contribution. The following are some of the factors considered:

- The Noble Not-for-Profit is providing services to individuals or organizations other than the local foundation.
- The resource provider determines the amount of payment.
- We do not have any indication that the Noble Not-for-Profit will incur economic penalties beyond the amount of payment for failure to perform.
- The Noble Not-for-Profit has control over the timing and place of services to be provided to third-party recipients.

2. The journal entries would be as follows:

- *The receipt of the grant award letter from the local foundation on May 15.*

| | | |
|---|---|---|
| Contributions receivable | $600,000 | |
| Contribution Revenue – Temporarily Restricted | | $600,000 |

- *The first advance of $50,000 foundation funds on July 15.*

| | | |
|---|---|---|
| Cash | $50,000 | |
| Contributions receivable | | $50,000 |

- *Reclassification of net asset amounts recorded on July 31.*

| | | |
|---|---|---|
| Temporarily Restricted Net Assets – Transfers Out | $70,000 | |
| Unrestricted Net Assets – Transfers In | | $70,000 |

**Note:** The preceding entry assumes that the Noble Not-for-Profit will spend restricted funds before unrestricted. However, if the grant requires that matching funds be spent simultaneously, then the preceding entry would change as follows:

| | | |
|---|---|---|
| Temporarily Restricted Net Assets – Transfers Out | $52,500 | |
| Unrestricted Net Assets – Transfers In | | $52,500 |

Solutions to Knowledge Check Questions

1.

    a. Correct. Useful indicators include the method of determining the amount of payment.

    b. Incorrect. Useful indicators include the penalties assessed if the not-for-profit fails to make timely delivery of assets.

    c. Incorrect. Useful indicators include the delivery of assets to be provided by the recipient not-for-profit.

    d. Incorrect. The auditor is not an indicator of any decision.

**2.**

    a. Correct. The time or place of delivery of the asset to be provided by the recipient not-for-profit to third-party recipients being at the discretion of the not-for-profit is indicative of a contribution.

    b. Incorrect. The method of delivery of the asset to be provided by the recipient not-for-profit to third-party recipients being specified by the resource provider is indicative of an exchange transaction.

    c. Incorrect. The resource provider determining the amount of the payment is indicative of a contribution.

    d. Incorrect. None of the indicators can override another. It must be based on facts.

**3.**

    a. Correct. The not-for-profit not being penalized for nonperformance is indicative of a contribution.

    b. Incorrect. The not-for-profit being penalized for nonperformance is indicative of an exchange transaction.

    c. Incorrect. Assets being delivered to individuals or organizations other than the resource provider are indicative of a contribution.

    d. Incorrect. None of the indicators can override another. It must be based on facts.

**4.**

    a. Correct. FASB ASC 958-605 discusses transactions in which foundations, business organizations, and other types of entities provide resources to not-for-profits under programs referred to as grants, awards, or sponsorships.

    b. Incorrect. If a not-for-profit has annual dues of $100 and the only benefit members receive is a monthly newsletter with a fair value of $25, $75 of the dues represents a contribution.

    c. Incorrect. Usually, the determination of whether membership dues are contributions rests on whether the value received by the member is commensurate with the dues paid.

    d. Incorrect. The determination of whether membership dues are contributions rests on whether the value received by the member is commensurate with the dues paid.

# Chapter 6

Case Study Solutions

## Contribution Revenues

Some procedures will address more than one assertion. Also, high risks of material misstatement may be able to be addressed in one procedure. It is important to note that the procedures do not represent equal amounts of time and that the procedures requiring the greatest amount of time address the higher risks of material misstatement.

## Sample Audit Plan for Contribution Revenue

### Audit Procedures for Payroll Deductions

| | |
|---|---|
| | 1. Have the client schedule the pledge amounts from payroll deductions by business by month for the current and future years. |
| Completeness | 2. Compare the businesses visited with those noted in the board minutes. If the client's schedule does not contain information for each business visited, instruct the client correct and resubmit. |
| Classification | 3. Review the National Giving form and note that it states clearly that contributions are for the general purposes of the organization. *If the auditor believes this is a moderate risk, the auditor may want to review forms signed by the employee for selected businesses to determine if there was any notation of a restriction on the contribution.* |
| Occurrence/ Cutoff | 4. Test the accuracy of the client's schedule by tracing the information to the forms from the businesses for X number of businesses. If client's schedule contains errors, instruct the client to correct the errors and resubmit the form. |
| Accuracy/ Cutoff | 5. Compare monthly pledged amounts to deposit from National Giving on bank statement for the following month. *If in prior years there have been no discrepancies noted, and there has been no change in the organization's personnel involved in this area or their procedures over this process, the auditor may compare amounts for X number of months rather than the entire year.* |

## Sample Audit Plan for Contribution Revenue

### Audit Procedures for Dinner, One-time Gifts, and Pledges

| | |
|---|---|
| Completeness | 1. Confirm with one or two board members that the schedule of envelopes was the schedule as presented to the board. Also, confirm the total number of envelopes with the board members. *This information may be available in the board minutes, and the auditor may want to refer to the minutes instead.* |
| Occurrence/ Accuracy/ Cutoff/ Classification | 2. Compare the amount of one-time gifts to the amount deposited from the dinner. |
| | 3. Have the client schedule the pledge amounts from the dinner by month for the current and future years. The schedule should include information noting which pledges remain outstanding at year-end. |
| Classification | 4. Review the pledge form used at the dinner and note that it states clearly that contributions are for the general purposes of the organization. *If the auditor believes this is a moderate risk, the auditor may want to review pledge forms to determine if there was any notation of a restriction on the contribution.* |
| Occurrence/ Cutoff | 5. Test the accuracy of the client's schedule by tracing the information to the pledge forms for X number of forms. Ensure that the pledges tested include three- and five-year pledges. If client's schedule contains errors, instruct the client to correct the errors and resubmit the form. |
| Accuracy | 6. Review the discount calculation for reasonableness. |
| Accuracy/ Cutoff | 7. For pledges greater than $X, trace current year pledge amounts to subsequent collection. *The auditor may expand this test to include a sample of pledges less than $X and should follow required documentation and procedures required when sampling.* |

**Pledges Receivable**

### Sample Audit Plan for Pledges Received

| | | |
|---|---|---|
| Existence/ Completeness | 1. | Consider the schedules obtained from the client during the audit procedures for contribution revenues. |
| Valuation | 2. | Compare monthly pledged amount outstanding at year-end to deposit from National Giving on bank statement for the following month. Investigate any uncollected amount. |
| Valuation | 3. | Review the amounts outstanding at year-end that were pledged to be paid by year-end. If significant, trace to subsequent collection. |
| Valuation | 4. | Consider length of delinquency of payment of pledges, amount of subsequent collections, and adequacy of valuation allowance. |
| Rights | 5. | Consider if there has been any indication of restriction on the organization's right to the pledge receivables. |
| Obligations | 6. | Consider if there are donor restrictions occurring but not being recognized. |

## Solutions to Knowledge Check Questions

**1.**

    a.  Incorrect. The audit team's understanding should include the organization's control environment or tone at the top.

    b.  Incorrect. The audit team's understanding should include the organization's process to identify business risks and how they address them.

    c.  Correct. The audit team's understanding of internal control should address financial reporting objectives and is not required to extend to operational objectives.

    d.  Incorrect. The audit team's understanding should include how the organization disseminates information and communicates to those both outside and inside the organization.

**2.**

    a.  Incorrect. Relevance is not an assertion, rather it is an attribute of audit evidence.

    b.  Incorrect. Occurrence and classification are assertions related to classes of transactions rather than account balances. Understandability is an assertion related to presentation and disclosure.

    c.  Correct. Existence, completeness, valuation, and rights and obligations are the assertions the auditor should consider for account balances.

    d.  Incorrect. Reliability is not an assertion, rather it is an attribute of audit evidence, and classifications are assertions related to classes of transactions.

**3.**

    a. Correct. Timeliness is not an assertion identified in generally accepted auditing standards.

    b. Incorrect. The audit team should consider cut-off as an assertion related to classes of transactions.

    c. Incorrect. The audit team should consider completeness as an assertion related to classes of transactions.

    d. Incorrect. The audit team should consider allocation as an assertion related to classes of transactions.

# CHAPTER 7

Case Study Solutions

| Item | Should the contributed service be recognized? If the service should be recognized, how might you value the service? |
|---|---|
| The normal duties of the treasurer | The UFNRV should not record contributed services for the normal duties of the treasurer. Although the current treasurer is a CPA and has specialized skills, the signing of checks and review of reconciliations does not require such skills and the organization would not normally purchase such services if they had not been contributed. |
| The treasurer's work on documenting internal controls | The UFNRV may or may not record contributed services for the treasurer documenting internal controls. It appears this task requires a specialized skill and the person has such skills. However, it is unclear whether the organization would normally purchase such services if they had not been contributed. If they would, the contributed services should be recorded. The services could be valued at the treasurer's normal billing rate. If the organization would not purchase such service, the services would not be recorded. |
| The football coach's speech | The UFNRV would probably not record contributed services for the football coach's speech. It is assumed that the organization would not normally purchase such services if they had not been contributed. However, if they would purchase this service, it would be recorded and valued at the speaker's normal rate. The speaker has specialized skills required for a kickoff event. |
| The labor to install the new roof on the building | The UFNRV should not record contributed services for the labor to install the new roof on the building. The services create or enhance a nonfinancial asset (for example, a building may be built or refurbished by volunteers); however, the asset is not owned by the UFNRV. They are leasing the building at no charge but have no formal lease or long-term commitment that would give rise to a leasehold improvement. |

Solutions to Knowledge Check Questions

**1.**

    a. Correct. Fair value should be used for the measure regardless of whether the not-for-profit could afford to purchase the services at their fair value.

    b. Incorrect. Contributed services that do not meet the criteria should not be recognized.

    c. Incorrect. Promises to give services that do not meet the criteria should not be recognized.

    d. Incorrect. Contributed services that meet the criteria are reported by not-for-profit organizations.

**2.**

    a. Correct. If a CPA contributes his or her services to a position that requires those skills and typically, the organization would have to pay for those services, it would be reported in the financial statements.

    b. Incorrect. If a CPA volunteers for an organization in a position that does not require his or her CPA skills or create or enhance a nonfinancial asset, it would not be reported in the financial statements.

    c. Incorrect. Just because an individual has a specialized skill does not mean that it meets the criteria to be reported.

    d. Incorrect. Only if a CPA contributes his or her services to a position that requires those skills and, typically, the organization would have to pay for those services, would it be reported in the financial statements.

**3.**

    a. Incorrect. There are disclosure requirements related to contributions of services.

    b. Incorrect. FASB ASC 958 provides examples of applying the accounting concepts related to contributed services.

    c. Correct. Contributed services should be recognized if employees of separately governed affiliated entities regularly perform services (in other than an advisory capacity) for and under the direction of the donee, and the recognition criteria for contributed services are met.

    d. Incorrect. Not-for-profits are encouraged to disclose contributed services that do not meet the recognition criteria.

# CHAPTER 8

Case Study Solutions

## Situation 1

1.

This is a revocable split-interest arrangement because "upon his death, his will may give the residual of the funds to the University."

2.

| Assets held in revocable agreements | $400,000 | |
|---|---|---|
| Refundable advances under revocable agreements | | $400,000 |

## Situation 2

1.

This is a charitable lead trust split-interest agreement. The board member states that: "Upon his death, the residual of the funds will go to the YWCA of Anywhere County."

2.

| Assets held in irrevocable agreements | $400,000 | |
|---|---|---|
| Liability under trust agreements | | $307,300 |
| Contribution revenue – temporarily restricted | | $ 92,700 |

## Solutions to Knowledge Check Questions

**1.**

   a.  Correct. The not-for-profit entity has an irrevocable right to receive the income earned on the trust assets in perpetuity.

   b.  Incorrect. The not-for-profit entity will never receive the assets held in trust.

   c.  Incorrect. A perpetual trust held by a third party is an agreement where the donor establishes a perpetual trust that will be administered by an individual or organization other than the not-for-profit entity.

   d.  Incorrect. A perpetual trust is not similar to a charitable gift annuity.

**2.**

   a.  Correct. A charitable remainder trust is an arrangement in which a donor establishes a trust with specified distributions to be made to a designated beneficiary or beneficiaries over the trust's term.

   b.  Incorrect. Upon termination of the trust, a not-for-profit entity receives the assets remaining in the trust.

   c.  Incorrect. Charitable remainder trusts are commonly used by not-for-profit entities.

   d.  Incorrect. The not-for-profit receives the remainder at the end of the trust.

**3.**

    a.   Incorrect. The agreements are similar to charitable remainder annuity trusts except that no trust exists.

    b.   Incorrect. The assets received are held as general assets of the not-for-profit entity.

    c.   Correct. The annuity liability is a general obligation of the organization.

    d.   Incorrect. The agreements are similar to charitable remainder annuity trusts except that no trust exists.

---

# CHAPTER 9

Case Study Solutions

Your assessment of the severity of this deficiency in internal control would be based on the effectiveness of the compensating controls performed by the board members. The compensating controls do not eliminate the deficiency but may mitigate the effects of the deficiency in internal control.

If the board member does not perform a review of the bank statement and the returned checks, verifying that all the checks have the appropriate signature and that the check payee and amount have not been altered, you might determine that the compensating control over disbursements is not effective in achieving the control objective and, therefore, a material weakness exists.

If the board member reviews only returned checks over a certain dollar amount, you might conclude that the compensating control is effective in preventing or detecting a material misstatement of cash and, therefore, this may be considered a significant deficiency because the magnitude of the reasonably possible misstatement is less than material.

However, if the board member examines the returned checks for the appropriate signature and alterations, and that board member is informed of the activities of the organization to allow the board member to identify something unexpected, you might conclude that the compensating control is effective in preventing or detecting an unauthorized disbursement, making the likelihood of a misstatement remote; therefore, this is only a deficiency in internal control and not a significant deficiency or material weakness.

Solutions to Knowledge Check Questions

**1.**

    a.   Incorrect. A system is affected by management but not outside vendors.

    b.   Incorrect. A system is affected by current personnel, but former personnel would no longer affect the system.

    c.   Incorrect. A system should not be affected by economic or industry factors.

    d.   Correct. A system is affected by those charged with governance.

**2.**

    a.   Incorrect. The auditor does not have to go looking for deficiencies in internal control.

    b.   Incorrect. Auditors are not required to design audit procedures specifically to detect deficiencies in internal control.

    c.   Incorrect. Auditors are required to report only control deficiencies that are significant deficiencies or material weaknesses.

    d.   Correct. The auditor may come across deficiencies in the performance of audit procedures.

**3.**

    a.   Correct. When the auditor comes across deficiencies, he or she is required to evaluate the deficiencies to assess severity and follow requirements to report the deficiencies to management and to those charged with governance.

    b.   Incorrect. In gaining an understanding of the organization's internal control, the auditor will typically identify deficiencies in the design or operation of internal control. Control deficiencies that do not rise to the level of significant deficiencies or material weaknesses are not required to be reported to management or to those charged with governance.

    c.   Incorrect. Testing internal control depends various factors, including the auditor's understanding of internal control, the auditor's expectations that internal control is likely to be effective, and the substantive evidence available to the auditor.

    d.   Incorrect. Deficiencies in the design are elements of the system of internal control where there is nothing to prevent or detect a misstatement or noncompliance. Deficiencies in the operation of the system of internal control is when it is not operating as designed.

**4.**

    a.   Incorrect. The severity of a deficiency does not depend on whether a misstatement actually occurred.

    b.   Correct. To the extent the financial statements include proposed adjustments by the auditor, the auditor needs to evaluate if there are reportable deficiencies.

    c.   Incorrect. The magnitude of a misstatement refers to its potential quantitative or qualitative materiality.

    d.   Incorrect. The auditor needs to consider beyond identified misstatements. The auditor needs to consider potential misstatements that could happen based on the design or operation of internal control.

**5.**

    a.   Incorrect. The auditor is not required to consider misstatements that the client corrected when evaluating deficiencies in internal control.

    b.   Incorrect. The auditor needs to consider potential misstatements that could happen based on the design of internal control, rather than those that could be prevented.

    c.   Incorrect. The auditor is responsible for considering misstatements that could happen based on the entity's internal control design.

    d.   Correct. The auditor needs to consider potential misstatements that could happen based on the design or operation of internal control.

**6.**

    a.   Correct. Risk factors include the susceptibility of the related asset or liability to loss or fraud.

    b.   Incorrect. The nature of the financial statement accounts, classes of transactions, disclosures, and assertions involved is a risk factor, not the internal controls implemented.

    c.   Incorrect. Risk factors include the possible future consequences of the deficiency but not future changes in the control.

    d.   Incorrect. Risk factors include the interaction or relationship of the control with other controls but not the relationship with generally accepted accounting principles.

**7.**

    a.   Correct. The auditor should determine whether deficiencies that affect the same significant account or disclosure, relevant assertion, or component of internal control collectively result in a significant deficiency or a material weakness.

    b.   Incorrect. The evaluation of whether a deficiency presents a reasonable possibility of misstatement may be made without quantifying the probability of occurrence as a specific percentage or range.

    c.   Incorrect. In many cases, the probability of a small misstatement will be greater than the probability of a large misstatement.

    d.   Incorrect. Deficiencies that affect the same account or disclosure should be considered together when evaluating the overall impact on the financial statements.

**8.**

    a.   Correct. The auditor's evaluation involves considering whether compensating controls exist.

    b.   Incorrect. The auditor should evaluate deficiencies found by the auditor or management, not management only.

    c.   Incorrect. Controls are not required to be tested for the auditor to evaluate a control deficiency.

    d.   Incorrect. Communication with governance may be a reporting requirement dependent on the conclusion of the auditor's evaluation of control deficiencies.

**9.**

    a.   Incorrect. Part of the thought process involves the auditor noting a potential deficiency, but there are other considerations.

    b.   Incorrect. Part of the thought process involves the auditor considering magnitude, but there are other considerations.

    c.   Incorrect. Part of the thought process involves the auditor considering likelihood, but there are other considerations.

    d.   Correct. All of the above are part of the evaluation process.

# CHAPTER 10

Case Study Solutions

| Question | Answer |
|---|---|
| What portion of the $40,000 costs related to the special fundraising event should be expensed? | The $25,000 spent on catering, promotional materials, and entertainment for the event should be expensed. The $15,000 spent on several exterior banners also should be expensed. Fundraising costs are expensed as incurred. Costs are incurred when the item or service has been received. |
| How would you prepare the journal entry for the 200 people who pledged $100 each to be paid within one year? | Based on past experience, the college expects to collect 95 percent of this amount. Contributions arising from unconditional promises to give that are expected to be collected within one year may be measured at their net realizable value. The entry would be:<br><br>dr. Contributions Receivable       $19,000<br>  cr. Contribution Revenue – Temporarily Restricted    $19,000<br><br>[**Note:** Some not-for-profits may use a subsidiary ledger to retain information concerning the $20,000 face amount of contributions promised in order to monitor collections of contributions promised.] |
| How would you prepare the journal entry for the twenty people who pledged $10,000 each to be paid in three years? | The college expects to collect 90 percent of this amount. The college estimates the present value to be $155,000. The entry would be:<br><br>dr. Contributions Receivable       $180,000<br>  cr. Contribution Revenue – Temporarily Restricted    $155,000<br>  cr. Discount on Contributions Receivable    $25,000<br><br>[**Note:** Similar to the preceding answer, some not-for-profits may use a subsidiary ledger to retain information concerning the $200,000 face amount of contributions promised in order to monitor collections of contributions promised.] |

Solutions to Knowledge Check Questions

1.
   a. Correct. Donations can take the form of cash.
   b. Incorrect. Donations can take the form of securities.
   c. Incorrect. Donations can take the form of land.
   d. Incorrect. Capital campaigns often last several years.

**2.**

    a.   Incorrect. Donations can take the form of buildings.

    b.   Correct. Donations can take the form of the use of facilities or utilities.

    c.   Incorrect. Donations can take the form of materials and supplies.

    d.   Incorrect. Capital campaigns often last several years.

**3.**

    a.   Incorrect. Donations can take the form of intangible assets.

    b.   Incorrect. Donations can take the form of services.

    c.   Correct. Donations can take the form of unconditional promises to give items in the future.

    d.   Incorrect. Capital campaigns often last several years, but do not have to last five years.

**4.**

    a.   Correct. Valuation techniques consistent with the market approach include matrix pricing and often use market multiples derived from a set of comparables.

    b.   Incorrect. The market approach uses prices and other relevant information generated by market transactions involving identical or comparable assets or liabilities.

    c.   Incorrect. Present value is not an exam of market approach.

    d.   Incorrect. The cost approach is not an example of a market approach.

# CHAPTER 11

Case Study Solutions

1.   It appears that membership fees would be contributions. The benefits to members are negligible.

2.   FNRT cannot report the net amount from the gala as a gain. Only activities that are peripheral or incidental to the organization can be reported as a gain. Because the gala will be an annual event and the amount is significant to the budget of the organization, this event is considered part of the organization's ongoing major activities. Revenue must be reported gross of any related expenses.

3.   The most that FNRT could report as contribution revenue from the gala is $9,000. This amount represents the $18,000 from ticket sales less the fair value of the event ($50 a person times 180 people).

4.   FNRT should report $1,180 as fundraising expense for the gala event. This consists of the $1,000 paid for invitations and the $180 paid for the key chains (a nominal gift for a contribution).

5.   The purchase of the projection system represents a transaction that is part exchange and part contribution. The projection system should be recorded at fair value as follows:

| | | |
|---|---|---|
| Equipment (projection system) | $15,000 | |
| Cash | | $ 5,000 |
| Contribution revenue | | $10,000 |

Solutions to Knowledge Check Questions

**1.**

    a.  Incorrect. Useful indicators include the duration of benefits.

    b.  Incorrect. Useful indicators include the expressed agreement concerning refundability of the payment.

    c.  Correct. Useful indicators include the qualifications for membership.

    d.  Incorrect. Useful indicators include extent of benefits.

**2.**

    a.  Incorrect. A request describing the dues as being used to provide benefits to the general public or to the not-for-profit's service beneficiaries is indicative of a contribution.

    b.  Incorrect. Negligible benefits to members is indicative of a contribution.

    c.  Correct. The not-for-profit providing service to members and nonmembers is indicative of a contribution.

    d.  Incorrect. The substantive benefits to members being available to nonmembers for a fee is indicative of an exchange transaction.

**3.**

    a.  Correct. An unspecified duration is indicative of a contribution.

    b.  Incorrect. Membership being available to the general public is indicative of a contribution.

    c.  Incorrect. Nonrefundable payment is indicative of a contribution. In exchange transaction criteria, benefits are provided for a defined period of time and additional payment of dues is required to extend member benefits.

    d.  Incorrect. The benefits being provided for a defined period is indicative of an exchange transaction.

---

# CHAPTER 12

Case Study Solutions

## Situation 1

1.

    Yes. The purpose, audience, and content criteria are met, and the joint costs should be allocated. (The costs of the second brochure should be charged to program because all the costs of the brochure are identifiable with the program function.)

    The activity calls for specific action by the recipient (exercising) that will help accomplish the not-for-profit's mission. The purpose criterion is met based on the other evidence, because (*a*) performing such programs helps accomplish Not-for-profit A's mission, and (*b*) the objectives of the program are documented in a letter to the public relations firm that developed the brochure.

    The audience criterion is met because the audience (residents over 65 in certain ZIP codes) is selected based on its need to use or reasonable potential for use of the action called for by the program component.

The content criterion is met because the activity calls for specific action by the recipient (exercising) that will help accomplish the not-for-profit's mission (increasing the physical activity of senior citizens), and the need for and benefits of the action are clearly evident (explains the importance of exercising).

2.

Yes. The purpose criterion is no longer met because a majority of compensation or fees for the fundraising consultant varies based on contributions raised for this discrete joint activity. All costs should be charged to fundraising, including the costs of the second brochure and any other costs that otherwise might be considered program or management and general costs if they had been incurred in a different activity.

## Situation 2

1.

The purpose, audience, and content criteria are not met. All costs should be charged to fundraising. The activity does not include a call for specific action because it only educates the audience about causes (describing the camp, its activities, who can attend, and the benefits to attendees). Therefore, the purpose criterion is not met.

The audience criterion is not met, because the audience is selected based on its ability or likelihood to contribute, rather than based on (a) its need to use or reasonable potential for use of the action called for by the program component, or (b) its ability to take action to assist the not-for-profit in meeting the goals of the program component of the activity. (Not-for-profit C believes that people in those neighborhoods would not need the camp's programs but may contribute.)

The content criterion is not met because the activity does not call for specific action by the recipient. (The content educates the audience about causes that the program is designed to address without calling for specific action.)

## Situation 3

1.

The purpose, audience, and content criteria are met, and the joint costs should be allocated.

The activity has elements of management and general functions. Therefore, no call for specific action is required. The purpose criterion is met based on the other evidence, because (a) the employees performing the activity are not members of the fundraising department and perform other non-fundraising activities and (b) internal management memoranda indicate that the purpose of the annual report is to fulfill one of the university's management and general responsibilities.

The audience criterion is met because the audience is selected based on its reasonable potential for use of the management and general component. Although the activity is directed primarily at those who have previously made significant contributions, the audience was selected based on its presumed interest in Not-for-profit D's annual report (prior donors who have made significant contributions are likely to have an interest in matters discussed in the annual report).

The content criterion is met because the activity (distributing annual reports) fulfills one of the entity's management and general responsibilities (reporting concerning management's fulfillment of its stewardship function).

Solutions to Knowledge Check Questions

**1.**

    a.   Correct. Examples of management and general activities include oversight.

    b.   Incorrect. Examples of management and general activities include business management.

    c.   Incorrect. Examples of management and general activities include soliciting revenue from exchange transactions.

    d.   Incorrect. Soliciting contributions from donors is an example of fundraising activities.

**2.**

    a.   Correct. The cost of oversight and management usually includes the salaries and expenses of the governing board.

    b.   Incorrect. The cost of oversight and management usually includes the salaries and expenses of the chief executive officer.

    c.   Incorrect. The cost of oversight and management usually includes the salaries and expenses of the supporting staff.

    d.   Incorrect. The costs of salaries and expenses of program managers is an example of program activities.

**3.**

    a.   Correct. Not-for-profit entities may solicit support through direct mail.

    b.   Incorrect. Not-for-profit entities may solicit support through telephone solicitation.

    c.   Incorrect. Not-for-profit entities may solicit support through door-to-door canvassing.

    d.   Incorrect. The cost of oversight is a management and general cost.

---

# CHAPTER 13

Case Study Solutions

## Situation 1

1.

Not-for-profit Z appears to meet the criteria of a voluntary health and welfare organization and therefore should present a statement of functional expenses.

Voluntary health and welfare organizations are required to present a statement of functional expenses. Voluntary health and welfare organizations are formed for the purpose of performing voluntary services for various segments of society. They are tax-exempt (organized for the benefit of the public), supported by the public, and operated on a "not-for-profit" basis. Most voluntary health and welfare organizations concentrate their efforts and expend their resources in an attempt to solve health and welfare problems of our society and, in many cases, those of specific individuals. As a group, voluntary health and welfare organizations include those not-for-profit entities that derive their revenue primarily from voluntary contributions from the general public to be used for general or specific purposes connected with health, welfare, or community services.

2.

The identification of risk factors for material misstatement and for fraud will vary by audit team and their understanding of the organization, its internal control, and its processes.

A quick analysis shows that fundraising expenses are 2½ percent of total expenses, and that management and general expenses are 9 percent of total expenses. The analysis also shows that payroll taxes and employee benefits as a percentage of payroll appears inconsistent for the functional classes. Considering the nature of the revenue of Not-for-profit Z, the following could be a few of the risk factors:

- Understatement of fundraising expenses, particularly payroll, payroll taxes and employee benefits, and occupancy.
- Understatement of management and general expenses.
- Allocation of payroll taxes and employee benefits among functional classifications.

3.

The audit team will develop audit procedures to test the following assertions for both the natural classification of expenses and the functional classification of expenses:

- Occurrence
- Completeness
- Accuracy
- Cutoff
- Classification

To obtain sufficient, appropriate evidence regarding the previously listed assertions, the audit team may include tests of functional classification of the following areas:

- Payroll and payroll taxes and employee benefits
- Professional services
- Supplies and equipment
- Occupancy

Based on the results of those tests, which address 93 percent of the total expenses, the audit team may consider the reasonableness of the remaining expenses based on their understanding of the costs included in those natural classifications and the functional allocation of them.

**Situation 2**

1.

Because Not-for-profit Z derives most of its revenue from fees for services, and not donations, Not-for-profit Z may not meet the criteria of a voluntary health and welfare organization and would not be required to present a statement of functional expenses. However, all not-for-profit entities are encouraged to do so.

If Not-for-profit Z does not present a statement of functional expenses, it would still be required to present the functional classifications of its expenses, either on the face of the statement of activities or in the notes.

2.

The identification of risk factors for material misstatement and for fraud will vary by audit team and their understanding of the organization, its internal control, and its processes.

A quick analysis shows management and general expenses are 9½ percent of total expenses. The analysis also shows that payroll taxes and employee benefits as a percentage of payroll appears inconsistent for the functional classes. It also shows that some of the natural expenses appear to have an even 10 percent allocation to management and general expenses. Considering the nature of the revenue of Not-for-profit Z, the following could be a few of the risk factors:

- Understatement of management and general expenses.
- Basis of allocation of management and general expenses.
- Allocation of payroll taxes and employee benefits among functional classifications.

3.

The audit team may include tests of functional classification of the following areas:

- Payroll and payroll taxes and employee benefits
- Professional services
- Occupancy, insurance, and training and development

Solutions to Knowledge Check Questions

1.
   a. Correct. Fundraising expenses are a functional classification and not a natural classification of expenses.
   b. Incorrect. A natural classification of expenses would include expense categories such as rent.
   c. Incorrect. A natural classification of expenses would include expense categories such as professional fees.
   d. Incorrect. A natural classification of expenses would include expense categories such as salaries.

2.
   a. Incorrect. The risk of fraudulent financial reporting of the *functional* classification of expenses is a consideration, but typically does not include the natural classification of expenses.
   b. Incorrect. The risk of material misstatement in classification due to error is a consideration related to the statement of functional expenses. The risk of material misstatement in completeness due to error is a consideration related to the statement of activities or the statement of financial position.
   c. Correct. The challenge of auditing estimates by management inherent to the statement of functional expenses is a consideration.
   d. Incorrect. The challenge of auditing complex calculations is a consideration, not immaterial balances.

**3.**

    a. Incorrect. Testing could involve reviewing supporting invoices for all professional services for occurrence, accuracy, cutoff, and natural classification.

    b. Correct. Testing typically does not involve comparing functional classification percentages with other organizations. Although this may provide management with information when competing for funding, it typically does not provide appropriate evidence for auditors.

    c. Incorrect. Testing could involve reviewing supporting invoices for legal services, audit fees, and clinician services for functional classification.

    d. Incorrect. Testing could involve determining total square footage of facilities affected by workplace design services.

# Chapter 14

Case Study Solutions

1. The solution to this scenario depends on how you break down the issues and whether you can or cannot support any value coming to Nika Sporting Goods Company.

   The first two items create a contribution of a facility regardless of the naming rights because the company cannot take back the facility. They also did not indicate that the college would be obligated to pay back any of the construction costs if the agreement is broken by either party.

   Items 3 and 4 do give the appearance of some value to Nika through national and international exposure through the broadcast of the bowl game with both the name of the stadium and the bowl game's name containing the company's name and logo. The additional funds to be paid after 25 years indicates some value placed on this agreement by the company to have the publicity (or advertising) of its name through the broadcast.

   Item five shows that the company has identified value for name recognition by providing for a contractual change through either a merger or acquisition.

   Item 6 appears to be a contribution of $500,000 restricted to the costs of running the bowl game. In addition, in the author's opinion, the $6,000,000 payment is an agency transaction whereby the college is acting as an intermediate or agent to transfer a contribution from the company to each institution whose team plays in the bowl game.

2. As to the tax issue, the unrelated business income (UBI) issue depends on whether the athletic events at the college meets the intent of the code for "Qualified Sponsorship Payment."

   You also have to review the issue of advertising as described in the code. A payment is not a qualified sponsorship payment if, in return, the organization advertises the sponsor's products or services.

   The final determination on the UBI issues is beyond this discussion but does give the reader a problem when considering the following from FIN 48 issues:

   FASB ASC 740-10-20 glossary: Tax Position

   A position in a previously filed tax return or a position expected to be taken in a future tax return that is reflected in measuring current or deferred income tax assets and liabilities for interim or annual periods. A tax position can result in a permanent reduction of income taxes payable, a deferral of income taxes otherwise currently payable to future years, or a change in the expected realizability of deferred tax assets. The term tax position also encompasses, but is not limited to

- a decision not to file a tax return,
- an allocation or a shift of income between jurisdictions,
- the characterization of income or a decision to exclude reporting taxable income in a tax return, and
- a decision to classify a transaction, entity, or other position in a tax return as tax exempt.

Solutions to Knowledge Check Questions

1.

    a.  Correct. The NFP should unbundle the transaction and determine the fair value of the contribution and exchange transaction components

    b.  Incorrect. The NFP should not consider this a contribution only.

    c.  Incorrect. The NFP should not consider this an exchange transaction only.

    d.  Incorrect. The NFP should not consider this miscellaneous revenue.

2.

    a.  Incorrect. Different guidance should not be followed when determining when to recognize revenue from an exchange transaction.

    b.  Correct. Revenues received from the exchange transaction component should be recorded consistent with exchange transaction recognition principles.

    c.  Incorrect. In some instances, some or all portions of an exchange transaction component could be deferred.

    d.  Incorrect. Exchange transactions should be recorded in a not-for-profit's financial statements.

# CHAPTER 15

Solutions to Knowledge Check Questions

1.

    a.  Incorrect. Although the auditor should be satisfied regarding the service auditor's professional competence and independence from the service organization and the adequacy of the standards under which the service auditor's report was issued, the other procedures are also required.

    b.  Incorrect. Although the auditor should inquire of the management of the user entity about whether the service organization has reported to the not-for-profit entity, or if management is otherwise aware of, any fraud, noncompliance with laws and regulations, or uncorrected misstatements affecting the financial statements, the other procedures are also required.

    c.  Incorrect. Although the auditor should evaluate the design and implementation of the not-for-profit entity's relevant controls that are applied to the transactions processed by the service organization, the other procedures are also required.

    d.  Correct. All of the above are required audit procedures regarding service organizations.

**2.**

    a.   Correct. The investment's primary purpose is to further the tax exempt objectives of the not-for-profit entity, and the asset is not expected to produce income or appreciate in value as a significant purpose.

    b.   Incorrect. The investment is not expected to produce income or appreciate in value.

    c.   Incorrect. The investment's primary purpose is to further the tax exempt objectives of the not-for-profit entity, and the asset is expected to produce income or appreciate in value.

    d.   Incorrect. The investment must have a contribution element.

**3.**

    a.   Incorrect. A group audit is an audit of group financial statements, regardless of how many audit organizations are involved.

    b.   Incorrect. The same audit organization may be both the group auditor and the component auditor.

    c.   Correct. Regardless of whether reference will be made to the component auditor's report, the group engagement team should obtain an understanding about whether the group engagement team will be able to obtain information affecting the consolidation process form a component auditor

    d.   Incorrect. If the group engagement partner chooses to make reference to the audit of the component auditor in the group auditor's report, there are a number of required audit procedures the group engagement partner and group engagement team should perform.

# Learn More

## AICPA CPE

Thank you for selecting AICPA as your continuing professional education provider. We have a diverse offering of CPE courses to help you expand your skillset and develop your competencies. Choose from hundreds of different titles spanning the major subject matter areas relevant to CPAs and CGMAs, including:

- Governmental & Not-for-Profit accounting, auditing, and updates
- Internal control and fraud
- Audits of Employee Benefit Plans and 401(k) plans
- Individual and corporate tax updates
- A vast array of courses in other areas of accounting & auditing, controllership, management, consulting, taxation, and more!

## Get your CPE when and where you want

- Self-study training options that includes on-demand, webcasts, and text formats with superior quality and a broad portfolio of topics, including bundled products like –
  - ➤ CPExpress for immediate access to hundreds of one and two-credit hour online courses for just-in-time learning at a price that is right
  - ➤ Annual Webcast Pass offering live Q&A with experts and unlimited access to the scheduled lineup, all at an incredible discount.
- Staff training programs for audit, tax and preparation, compilation and review
- Certificate programs offering comprehensive curriculums developed by practicing experts to build fundamental core competencies in specialized topics
- National conferences presented by recognized experts
- Affordable AICPA courses on-site at your organization – visit **aicpalearning.org/on-site** for more information.
- Seminars sponsored by your state society and led by top instructors. For a complete list, visit **aicpalearning.org/publicseminar**.

## Take control of your career development

The AICPA I CIMA Competency and Learning website at **https://competency.aicpa.org** brings together a variety of learning resources and a self-assessment tool, enabling tracking and reporting of progress toward learning goals.

### Visit the AICPA store at **cpa2biz.com/CPE** to browse our CPE selections.

**AICPA®** Governmental Audit Quality Center

# Governmental audits have never been more challenging.

## Are you with a CPA firm or state auditor office? If so, join the Governmental Audit Quality Center and get the support, information and tools you need. Save time. Maximize audit quality. Enhance your practice.

For 10 years, the GAQC has committed to helping firms and state audit organizations (SAOs) achieve the highest quality standards as they perform financial statement audits of government, single audits, HUD audits or other types of compliance audits. If you are not yet a member, consider joining the GAQC to maximize your audit quality and practice success!

Join online today at gaqc.aicpa.org/memberships and start on the path to even greater audit success. Membership starts at just $190 (for firms or SAOs with fewer than 10 CPAs).

## Benefits at a glance
### The GAQC offers:

- **Email alerts** with audit and regulatory updates

- A dedicated **website (aicpa.org/GAQC)** where you can network with other members

- Access to Resource Centers on Single Audits (both under the new Uniform Guidance for Federal Awards and OMB Circular A-133), *Government Auditing Standards*, HUD topics, GASB Matters and much more

- Audit Practice Tools and Aids (e.g., GASB's new pension standards, internal control documentation tools, schedule of expenditures of federal awards practice aids, Yellow Book independence documentation practice aid, etc.)

- Savings on **professional liability insurance**

- A **website listing** as a firm or SAO committed to quality, which makes your information available to the public and/or potential purchasers of audit services

- Exclusive **webcasts** on timely topics relevant to governmental financial statement audits and compliance audits (optional CPE is available for a small fee, and events are archived online)

### Topics the GAQC webcasts cover include:

- Auditor Planning for the New Uniform Guidance for Federal Awards

- GASB Pension Standards

- An Overview of the Latest OMB Compliance Supplement

- Audit Quality Series Avoiding Common Deficiencies

- HUD's Audit Requirements

- Planning Considerations for your Governmental and NPO Audits

- Don't be the last to Know — Fraud in the Governmental Environment

- Yellow Book and Single Audit Fundamentals

**To learn more about the Governmental Audit Quality Center,** its membership requirements or to apply for membership, visit aicpa.org/GAQC, email us at gaqc@aicpa.org or call us at 202.434.9207.

 CPExpress

# Just-in-time learning at your fingertips 24/7

Where can you get <u>unlimited online access</u> to 900+ credit hours (650+ CPE courses) for one low annual subscription fee?

**CPExpress**, the AICPA's comprehensive bundle of online continuing professional education courses for CPAs, offers you immediate access to hundreds of one and two-credit hour courses. You can choose from a full spectrum of subject areas and knowledge levels to select the specific topic you need when you need it for just-in-time learning.

**Access hundreds of courses for one low annual subscription price!**

How can CPExpress help you?

- ✓ Start and finish most CPE courses in as little as 1 to 2 hours with 24/7 access so you can fit CPE into a busy schedule
- ✓ Quickly brush up or get a brief overview on hundreds of topics when you need it
- ✓ Create and customize your personal online course catalog for quick access with hot topics at your fingertips
- ✓ Print CPE certificates on demand to document your training – never miss a CPE reporting deadline!
- ✓ Receive free Quarterly updates – Tax, Accounting & Auditing, SEC, Governmental and Not-For-Profit

## Quantity Purchases for Firm or Corporate Accounts
If you have 10 or more employees who require training, the Firm Access option allows you to purchase multiple seats. Plus, you can designate an administrator who will be able to monitor the training progress of each staff member. To learn more about firm access and group pricing, visit aicpalearning.org/cpexpress or call 800.634.6780.

## To subscribe, visit **cpa2biz.com/cpexpress**

# Why AICPA?

## Think of All the Great Reasons to Join the AICPA.

**CAREER ADVOCACY SUPPORT**

On behalf of the profession and public interest on the federal, state and local level.

**PROFESSIONAL & PERSONAL DISCOUNTS**

Save on travel, technology, office supplies, shipping and more.

**ELEVATE YOUR CAREER**

Five specialized credentials and designations (ABV®, CFF®, CITP®, PFS™ and CGMA®) enhance your value to clients and employers.

**HELPING THE BEST AND THE BRIGHTEST**

AICPA scholarships provide more than $350,000[1] to top accounting students.

**GROW YOUR KNOWLEDGE**

Discounted CPE on webcasts, self-study or on-demand courses & more than 60 specialized conferences & workshops.

**PROFESSIONAL GUIDANCE YOU CAN COUNT ON**

Technical hotlines & practice resources, including Ethics Hotline, Business & Industry Resource Center and the Financial Reporting Resource Center.

**KEEPING YOU UP TO DATE**

With news and publications from respected sources such as the *Journal of Accountancy.*

**MAKING MEMBERS HAPPY**

We maintain a 94%+ membership renewal rate.

**FOUNDED ON INTEGRITY**

Representing the profession for more than 125 years.

**RELATIONSHIPS THAT COUNT**
Over 400,000 Members in 145 Countries

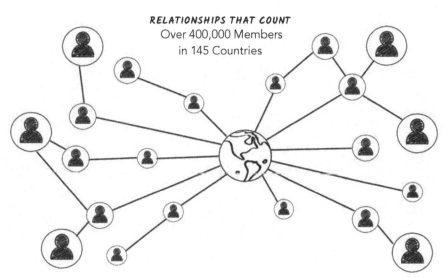

**TO JOIN, VISIT:**
aicpa.org/join or call 888.777.7077.